AUTHOR
OF
ALMIGHTY GOD'S
LAST TESTAMENT
TO
➤ ALL ◄ MANKIND
IS
THE "CREATOR"

ARCHWAY
PUBLISHING

Archway Publishing books may be ordered through booksellers or by contacting:

Archway Publishing
1663 Liberty Drive
Bloomington, IN 47403
www.archwaypublishing.com
1-(888)-242-5904

ISBN: 978-1-4808-0455-5 (sc)
ISBN: 978-1-4808-0454-8 (e)

Library of Congress Control Number: 2013922253

Printed in the United States of America

Archway Publishing rev. date: 12/17/13

"ALMIGHTY God's"
LAST TESTAMENT
TO
→ALL← MANKIND

Tells "THOSE" who read this Testament containing "THREE" Packets will give them to "PONDER" a "FEW" of "LIFES→MYSTERIES←" →SUCH AS←

The "END TIME" Revelation of Almighty Gods →"TWO"← Present Day →WITNESSES← How they were CHOSEN, TRAINED, DIRECTED, & USED BY Almighty God for 30+ YEARS to give→"HIM"← everything →"NEEDED"← to fulfill →HIS← PROMISE to "ABRAHAM" giving the "JEWS" their →"WAY"← to find "SALVATION" through the "TRANSUBSTANTIATION"

PACKET #1

Contains a number of "__LETTERS__" directed to those ecclesiastics holding positions of authority within the Church that was founded by Jesus Christ on Peter that became the "__Roots__" responsible to "__USE__" →"__H-I-S__"← "TWO" __WITNESSES__ in a "__LAST__" __DITCH__ attempt to get →"__H-I-S__"← Church back on "__TRACK__".

PACKET #2

Contains a number of "__LETTERS__" regarding "__Almighty Gods__" "TWO" __END TIME__ Witnesses that were →"__H-I-S__"← __ONLY MEANS__ of returning to this "__LAND__" of →"__EXILE__"←

TO VENT →"H-I-S"← →WRATH← in a →"Human"← WAY making it →"POSSIBLE" for →"ALL"← who →READ←

ALMIGHTY GOD'S
LAST TESTAMENT
TO
→ALL← MANKIND

With an OPEN DOOR in their →"MIND'S"← →WILL← be →GIVEN← to →READ← the →"S-P-O-K-E-N"← →"MIND"← of →"ALMIGHTY← GOD← that →"WAS"← →PENNED"←→"WORD BY WORD"← through →"ONE"← of →"H-I-S"← →"TWO"← →"Witnesses"←
→as well as←

Reading of the →"TOTAL"← collapse of the World System that →"H-A-D"← !!!!!!! →"BEEN"← held together BY →"Almighty God"← in the

"LETTER" of →"PROCLAMITION"←

PACKET #3

One of which →"REVEALS"← Almighty God's Humaness & ability to →"LASH"← out in present day language to those ecclesiasites who have →"DESTROYED"← →H-I-S← Church

→ as well as ←

The →F-I-N-A-L← Chapter in the "WORLD" Giving →"ALL"← mankind to "KNOW" more About "Almighty Gods" present day →End "TIME"← & →MUCH LOVED← "TWO" Witnesses.

& →"L-A-S-T-L-Y"←

The Genisis of the God/Man.

PACKET #1

June 6th, 2007.

Jacob Neusner

"T-I-M-E" has given to "T-W-O" who are being "M-O-V-E-D" by "O-N-E" the "WAY" to "FIND" the "J-E-W" WHO "H-A-S" been chosen by (Almighty "GOD") to BECOME (the "O-N-E" & "O-N-L-Y" "J-E-W") to whom WILL be made known the "MYSTERY" surrounding the "P-E-R-S-O-N" named "Jesus"

Jacob Neusner

"UN" like "ALL" "J-E-W-S" chosen by (Almighty "G-O-D") "YOUR" calling is "ONE" in which "Y-O-U" Jacob Neusner "W-I-L-L" receive "KNOWLEDGE" regarding "GOD'S" promised message of "S-A-L-V-A-T-I-O-N" for "YOUR" people THE "JEWS" making it "P-O-S-S-I-B-L-E" to "F-O-R-G-I-V-E" "T-H-E-M" for their "M-I-S-D-E-E-D-S" to "O-N-E" called "Jesus Christ".

Jacob Neusner

Almighty "God" Has →"R-E-A-C-H-E-D"← that POINT in "T-I-M-E" where in "HE" is _now_ "L-O-O-K-I-N-G" to _"THOSE"_ "S-C-H-O-L-A-R-L-Y" individuals _WHO_ →"B-E-L-I-E-V-E"← _like_ Jacob in →_their_← →"GOD"← as _ONE_ who becomes the →"E-P-I-T-O-M-E"← of _ALL_ we fashion →"O-U-R"← _Messiah_ to be making →_"YOUR"_← _"T-A-S-K"_ of coming to GRIPS with →"REALITY"← one, in which →"_you_"← will require a _firmness of purpose_ should →"Y-O-U"← Jacob Neusner elect to _"PURSUE"_ the →"P-O-S-S-I-B-I-L-I-T-Y"← that "TWO" hold the "KEY" that "U-N" _locks_ the "D-O-O-R" in _your_ "MIND" to a "W-O-R-L-D" wherein _Almighty_ →"GOD"← makes known to →"THOSE"← "HE" has "CHOSEN" "P-R-O-O-F" beyond

"A-L-L" doubt the "GENUINENESS" of "T-W-O" (present-"D-A-Y") "O-R-A-C-L-E-S" belonging to "O-N-E" should the "S-E-L-F" force "CONTROLLING" Jacob "ELECT" to "L-I-S-T-E-N" rather than "S-C-R-E-W" Up "like" so "M-A-N-Y" "M-A-N-Y" who "N-E-V-E-R" "L-O-O-K-E-D" beyond their "own" "S-E-L-F" importance to give "any" "C-R-E-D-E-N-C-E" to "T-W-O" "unknown" "L-A-Y" "personalities" "WHO" were being moved by "ONE" in a "L-A-S-T" ditch "ATTEMPT" to "BROADEN" their "SPIRITUAL" "S-C-O-P-E" through "LISTENING" to "TWO" "WHO" were "GIVEN" the "I-M-P-O-S-S-I-B-L-E" "TASK" of dealing with "C-L-O-S-E-D" minds as "E-V-I-D-E-N-C-E-D" by the "M-A-N-N-E-R" in which "THEY" the recipients "L-O-O-K-E-D"

ON "B-O-T-H" the ("CONTENTS" & "AUTHOR") of the "L-E-T-T-E-R-S" "attached" as coming from "O-N-E" whose "MIND" is still "circling" for a landing "W-I-T-H" the "EXCEPTION" of "ONE" who gave "C-R-E-D-E-N-C-E" to the "ONE" responsible for moving "HIM" to "C-O-M-P-L-Y" with the "THREAT" of "M-I-S-F-O-R-T-U-N-E" thus KEEPING "S-A-F-E" Almighty "G-O-D-S" promise to "A-B-R-A-H-A-M".

Jacob Neusner

"U-N-L-E-S-S" we become "MORE" pragmatic in our endeavours to "SEARCH" for "T-R-U-T-H" "outside" the "B-A-R-R-I-E-R" called "T-I-M-E" & "ACCEPT" the "C-A-L-L-I-N-G" "OFFERED" "you" By "O-N-E" whom Jacob "B-E-L-I-E-V-E-S" is "Y-E-T" to "C-O-M-E" "despite" the

"M-A-N-N-E-R" in which →"you"← set "A-B-O-U-T" to →"PROVE"← to (your "S-E-L-F") unequivocally using Jacobs "S-E-L-F" taught "ACUMEN" to "D-I-S-C-E-R-N" that the "O-N-E" "C-A-L-L-E-D" "Jesus Christ" was "NOTHING" more than "M-A-N" leaving Jacob to "P-O-N-D-E-R" the "C-A-L-L-I-N-G" "O-F-F-E-R-E-D" by Almighty "G-O-D" to Jacob Neusner the "ONE" & "ONLY" "J-E-W" "CHOSEN" the "A-N-S-W-E-R" to the "M-Y-S-T-E-R-Y" surrounding the "G-O-D" "M-A-N" Almighty "G-O-D"

August 21st, 1991.

Father Franz Schmidberger

Would you believe a stranger were he to write _suggesting_ that the Pharisaical approach practiced by the →"_remnant_"← of the Universal Catholic Church ≡"_remaining_"≡ called the Society of St. Pius X →_will_← suffer a similar fate to that of the Pharisees during Christ's time here on earth →"_unless_"← you change your mental outlook & those of your _whole_ priestly society ???

Father Franz Schmidberger
* Would you believe a stranger were he to write _suggesting_ that _Almighty_ God _does_ ≡"_not_"≡ !!!!!!! with-hold Himself

from _anyone_ for the sole reason
their ~dress~ _fails_ to measure up to
~"_HIS_"~ !!! liking ???

*** Father Franz Schmidberger
   Would you believe a stranger were
he to write _suggesting_ that _Almighty God_
~"surely"~ had "_your_" society in mind
when Jesus _was moved_ to cite the
case history of a bunch of ~"_blind_"~
religious _overbearing_ ~"_hypocrites_"~
called pharisees who believed ~_like you_~
in _all_ matters pertaining to morals
& (~_church Law_~) _controlling_ the _laity_ ???

   Father Franz Schmidberger
Would you believe a stranger were HE
to ~"_tell_"~ you that your _preconceived_

ideas concerning <u>Almighty</u> God's
make up <u>guarantees</u> that "<u>HE</u>" will
<u>for "EVER"</u> remain a mystery ???

Father Franz Schmidberger
Would you believe a stranger were "HE"
to "<u>tell</u>" you that <u>Almighty</u> God
"<u>does not</u>" like being "<u>W-I-E-L-D-E-D</u>"
<u>about</u> by a bunch of <u>hypocritical</u>
"Q-U-A-C-K-S" who call themselves
priests of the <u>Society of St. Pious "X"</u>
founded by a <u>Rebel Prelate</u> named
<u>Marcel Lefebvre</u> who found "<u>favour</u>"
with <u>Almighty</u> God for "<u>K-E-E-P-I-N-G</u>"
"<u>Alive</u>" the covenant made by "GOD"
to Abraham to give to "<u>HIS</u>" people
their way to find "<u>salvation</u>"
through the "<u>TRUE</u>" Sacrificial Offering

bestowed by Jesus Christ to a bunch of "Jews" (the "Apostles") which has been kept "S-A-F-E" (for "them") for nigh on TWO thousand years by the ("Roman Catholic Church") who "L-O-O-K-E-D" on it as "THEIRS" !!! when in retrospect they are "NOTHING" more than the guardians given the "SOUL saving" opportunity of "benefiting" through protecting it for Almighty God that "His" end TIME PROMISE for → "HIS" ← people the "JEWS" would be "kept" which Father Franz Schmidberger should?? give you & your ilk to "ponder" How ("very little") you really do comprehend about the "WAYS" of Almighty God.

** Father Franz Schmidberger

Would you believe a stranger were "HE" to →"tell"← you that Almighty God →"N-E-V-E-R"← excuses →"O-R"← !!!!!!! forgives those WHO take it on them→"S-E-L-V-E-S"← to →"B-U-R-D-E-N"← the faithful →"U-S-I-N-G"← Almighty "GOD" to A-C-H-I-E-V-E their purpose.

**** Father Franz Schmidberger
like Marcel Lefebvre you tend to →"B-L-I-N-D"← !!! your→"S-E-L-F"← to the →"T-R-U-T-H"← in →"A-L-L"← that has been →"D-I-S-C-L-O-S-E-D"← over the past→"D-E-C-A-D-E"← through letters from a →"S-T-R-A-N-G-E-R"← who →"W-A-S"← the →"P-A-N-A-C-E-A"← for that which →"troubled"← a "weak" "unobtrusive" "indecisive" "timid" personality who would →"N-O-T"← through

mortal "F-E-A-R" let go of the "Self" F-O-R-C-E blinding HIM" to a Church "B-O-D-Y" responsible for "D-E-S-T-R-O-Y-I-N-G" its "S-E-L-F" by placating a "D-I-S-S-I-D-E-N-T" bunch of "S-E-C-T-S" that W-I-L-L "never" change "B-E-C-A-U-S-E" Father Schmidberger your "M-E-N-T-O-R" still "L-O-C-K-E-D" on him "S-E-L-F" as belonging in "M-I-N-D" to that Church "B-O-D-Y" which had ("C-O-N-D-I-T-I-O-N-E-D" it) making the "T-A-S-K" of "D-E" programming one "W-H-O" "thinks" "acts" "believes" & "behaves" in a similar fashion to ("T-H-O-S-E" governing) in the Church "B-O-D-Y" that had to be "C-U-T" away Father Franz Schmidberger in order to "keep" "B-O-T-H" Almighty "GOD'S" promised

message of "S-A-L-V-A-T-I-O-N" to Abraham "U-N" tainted -"&"- fulfill Holy Scripture <u>required</u> the "U-S-E" of an <u>"INSTRUMENT"</u> in the form of a Stranger <u>who</u> "B-E-L-I-E-V-E-S" after a <u>"D-E-C-A-D-E"</u> of putting up with a <u>"B-U-N-C-H"</u> of <u>"blind"</u> <u>"stupid"</u> <u>overbearing</u> <u>"hypocritical</u> <u>Quacks</u> with <u>closed</u> "M-I-N-D-S" has left this individual with <u>"N-O"</u> alternative other than to ("V-I-E-W" <u>the SOCIETY</u>) of which -"<u>you</u>"- Father Franz Schmidberger are its Superior as

(AN "<u>E-X-E-R-C-I-S-E IN FUTILITY</u>")

Amen

cc / Bishop Richard Williamson <u>NB</u> * * * *
Father Jacques Emily <u>NB</u> * *, *, * * *
Father Gerard Rusak <u>NB</u> *

July 26th, 1982.

Archbishop Marcel Lefebvre
In "OUR" ABANDONMENT of "ALL" that "WE"
"TENACIOUSLY" embraced DURING a crucial
PERIOD in the "LIFE" of "GOD'S" Church
"WE" SURRENDER to "ONE" WHO HAS
"PLOTTED" AGAINST "GOD" to "PREVENT"
that WHICH "GOD" MADE POSSIBLE for
"MAN" through the "CRUCIFICTION & DEATH
of His ONLY "SON" Jesus Christ "SALVATION

Archbishop Marcel Lefebvre in
"OUR" ABANDONMENT of "ALL" "WE" previously
"STRUGGLED" to RETAIN "WE" SURRENDER the
"ONE" SEGMENT "STILL" remaining of the
"DESOLATE DEBRIS" that is called the
"LIVING" Church to PROVIDE a "WAY" the "ONLY
SURE WAY "WE" can be "ASSURED" of

2

FINDING "SALVATION".

Archbishop Marcel Lefebvre in "OUR" ABANDONMENT of "ALL" "WE" VOWED to KEEP "SAFE" "WE" become "ANSWERABLE" to "GOD" for "ALL" THOSE "confused" SOULS WHO are "DESPERATELY" attempting to DISCERN the "ACTIONS" of the "Spiritual" HEAD of a rebellious "LITTLE BAND" that "INITIALLY" PERFORMED in a manner "MOST" pleasing to "GOD".

Archbishop Marcel Lefebvre "WHY" do WE "SEEK" to "UNBURDEN" "OUR" PLIGHT to "ONE" "WHO" is "most" DECEITFUL in his manner of MISLEADING "US" into "BELIEVING" "HE" "IS" "ONE" INDIVIDUAL "WHO" CHAMPIONS "OUR" MOVEMENT WHILE "simultaneously" "CONSPIRING" "YOUR" DOWNFALL.

3

<u>Archbishop</u> Marcel Lefebvre "<u>WHY</u>" do "WE" "<u>Look</u>" "to" "ONE" <u>WHO IS</u> considered by a "<u>NUMBER</u>" of the "<u>ECCLESTICAL</u>" OLD GUARD remaining in the "<u>INNER SANCTUM</u>" of "GOD'S" Church to be an "<u>ADVERSARY</u>" of "<u>TRADITIONAL DOGMA</u>" be expected to <u>GIVE</u> "YOU" a <u>FAIR SHAKE</u> .

<u>Archbishop</u> Marcel Lefebvre "WITHOUT" the "<u>HELP</u>" of "GOD" it becomes <u>IMPOSSIBLE</u> for "<u>US</u>" to distinguish the <u>PRECISE</u> "ROUTE" "<u>WE</u>" <u>are</u> to "NAVIGATE" the ONLY "TRUE" segment of GOD'S Church still standing "DESPITE" the <u>ONSLAUGHT</u> "<u>CREATED</u>" by satans <u>penetration</u> of the <u>ecclesiastical</u> "BODY" of the "INNER SANCTUM" of the Church that <u>WAS</u> founded by Jesus Christ "<u>ON</u>"!!! (<u>PETER</u>) "WHO" <u>VIEWED</u> <u>them</u>"<u>SELVES</u>" as a <u>BUNCH</u> of

4

"LATTER DAY" APOSTLES ("DIVINELY") chosen THAT are in "RETROSPECT" "NOTHING" more than Religious "MEMBERS" of the Church "SELECTED" for a REASON ??? & elevated to the RANK of "BISHOP" by the PRESIDING →"VICAR" of Christ that "HAS" caused the GREAT "SCHISM" "WE" are experiencing "TO-DAY" following VATICAN II necessitating "US" to BECOME most "PRAGMATIC" in "OUR" thinking "LEST" "WE" "LOSE" that which "WE" Marcel Lefebvre "STRIVED" so diligently to "UPHOLD".

Should "you" Archbishop Marcel Lefebvre remain "STEADFAST" in "YOUR" RESOLVE to shortly "ABANDON for "FEAR" of becoming "ENMESHED" in a "SPIRITUAL QUARREL" with "THOSE" in the "FRATERNITY" ADAMANT in their "REBELLIOUSNESS"

to "CONTRAVENE" DOCTRINAL LAW Pre VATICAN II the "only" TRUE segment of the Church remaining that WAS founded by Jesus Christ "ON" !!! (PETER) "MUST" ANSWER to "GOD" for "ALL" THOSE confused "SOULS" desperately "ATTEMPTING" to "DISCERN" the "TRUTH" Archbishop Marcel Lefebvre "AMIDST" the "GROWING" anxiety of "MANY" "ADHERENTS" perceiving a "MOVEMENT" "NOT" dissimilar in "IT'S" concept to the "MODE" employed by "THOSE" in the "UNIVERSAL" Church "WHO" WILL also "be" MADE to "STAND" before "GOD" to "GIVE" count of "THEIR" WICKED CRIMES against "GOD" WHICH HAS Archbishop Lefebvre "CAUSED" !!! the "UN" COUNTABLE "LOSS" of "SOULS" "DISPERSED" for "ALL" time .

Archbishop "Marcel Lefebvre" the "TASK" of

6

"SAFEGUARDING" the "REMAINS" of "GOD'S" Church "REQUIRES" a firmness of "PURPOSE" WHICH "can" "ONLY" come from "THOSE" "WHO" are "truly" "DEDICATED" to "GOD" believing "He" WILL "through" CONSCIENCE tell "you" Archbishop Marcel Lefebvre "THAT" which is "contrary" to what "SELF" "may" DECREE "concealing" "our" TRUE "FEELING" in "REFUSING" to "ACCEPT" "THAT" "WHICH OUR" CONSCIENCE" "IS" DICTATING "SOLELY" because "it" FAILS to measure "UP" to "YOUR" !!! "HUMAN" Standards of "ACCEPTABILITY"

"GOD" Archbishop "Marcel Lefebvre" does "NOT" "ACT" in a "MANNER" suitable to "YOUR" "SCOPE" of "COMPREHENSION" "therefore" "IT" becomes "MOST" necessary for "YOU" to "RELY" "ON" YOUR "GOD" given common "SENSE" !!! to "DISCERN" & "FULFILL" "ALL" that "YOUR"

"GOD" given "CONSCIENCE" "IS" "TELLING YOU".

September 8th, 1986.

Archbishop Marcel Lefebvre

Like "S.O" M-A-N-Y others who "H-A-V-E" NOT "listened" to "TWO" individuals solely "B-E-C-A-U-S-E" "THEY" were what "you" Marcel would "L-O-O-K" down your "N-O-S-E" on rendering it "I-M-P-O-S-S-I-B-L-E" to "F-I-N-D" what "L-I-F-E" has "P-R-O-M-I-S-E-D" "U-N-T-I-L" the "DAY" "A-R-C-H-B-I-S-H-O-P"!!!

Marcel Lefebvre "S-T-O-O-P-S" to the "L-E-V-E-L" of the "U-N" sophisticated WHO Scripture "R-E-V-E-A-L-S" Almighty "GOD" "P-I-C-K-S" as "HIS"!!! medium to "confound" the "KNOW IT ALLS" that (F-O-R "ever") "SCREW U-P" & "L-I-S-T-E-N-S" with an ("O-P-E-N" mind) to "TWO" WHO are for the "L-A-S-T" T-I-M-E !!!!!!!!!!!!!

being →"M-O-V-E-D"← to →"ASK"← "A-R-C-H-B-I-S-H-O-P"
Marcel Lefebvre →"WHY"← !!! do →"SO"← many
→"F-A-I-L"← !!!! to "FIND" the S-O-L-U-T-I-O-N
to that which causes them D-I-S-T-R-E-S-S
→"WHY"← !!! do →"SO"← many →"F-A-I-L"← !!!! to
"receive" from "LIFE" that which
they "S-E-E-K" ?

Marcel →"E-V-E-R-y"← thing "WE" need to
fulfill "U-S" for "OUR" particular →"NICHE"←
in ("LIFE'S" →plan←) is "O-F-F-E-R-E-D" to →"ALL"
"WHO" overcome the →"S-E-L-F"← force
responsible for K-E-E-P-I-N-G "US"
"OUT"side of "LIFE'S" protective custody
"U-N-T-I-L" WE accept the "N-E-E-D" to "L-O-O-K"
with an "O-P-E-N" door in the mind
rather than ALLOW →"self"← to
("P-R-E-J-U-D-I-C-E" →you←) like →"S-O"← M-A-N-y←
others that placed their →"S-E-L-F"← esteem

→"B-E-Y-O-N-D"← the →"R-E-A-C-H"← of →any "ONE"← ("L-I-F-E" is using) to get "HIS" message across simply because →"T-H-E-Y"← too →"C-L-O-S-E-D"← their minds.

Archbishop Marcel Lefebvre →"U-N-T-I-L"← "YOU" (→stop← "L-O-O-K-I-N-G") for →"D-I-R-E-C-T-I-O-N"← from Almighty "GOD" in some →"U-N-"!!! worldly →manner← & →"S-T-A-R-T"← using →"common"← S-E-N-S-E →"L-I-F-E"← cannot (→"H-E-L-P"← "you") !!!!

Archbishop Marcel Lefebvre →"U-N-T-I-L"← "YOU" (→stop← & "R-E-F-L-E-C-T") O-N the →manner← !!!!!!!!!!!! in W-H-I-C-H Jesus Christ →"GOD"←/man →"A-P-P-E-A-R-E-D"← to "P-O-I-N-T" the →"WAY"← to a "WORLD" beyond by using a →"N-A-T-U-R-A-L"← medium "with" an →"O-P-E-N"← door in the mind

→"L-I-F-E"← cannot (→"H-E-L-P"← "you"-)!!!!

Archbishop Marcel Lefebvre like→"S-O"
M-A-N-Y← others "WHO"→F-A-I-L-E-D← to
place→any← C-R-E-D-E-N-C-E that
Almighty "GOD" would→"S-P-E-L-L"-out
"HIS" message to "ONE" in→their-"P-O-S-I-T-I-O-N"
on the "E-C-C-L-E-S-I-A-S-T-I-C-A-L LADDER" of
GOD'S church by "U-S-I-N-G"→"TWO"←
→"U-N" known←→"U-N" sophisticated← worldly
forms "T-A-K-E-N" Marcel from the
(→T-I-M-E← period) "WE" LIVE →in← to
become the→"H-A-R-B-I-N-G-E-R"← of the
→"S-P-O-K-E-N WORD"← simply because
→"THEY"← too→"C-L-O-S-E-D"← their→"minds"←
to "ANY" possibility that "GOD" would
→come "AGAIN"← in a→"H-U-M-A-N"← way.

5

Archbishop Marcel Lefebvre "L-I-F-E" HAS
given to "ONE" currently in a "POSITION"
held to be responsible for "SAFEGUARDING
the "D-O-C-T-R-I-N-A-L" remains of Gods
Church "THREE" letters together with
"C-O-P-I-E-S" of letters "D-I-R-E-C-T-E-D" to
John Paul II Cardinal Agostino Casaroli
Archbishop Joseph Glemp & the REMAINING
member of the (→"FATIMA"← incident) →"ALL"←
of which have been re copied & herewith
enclosed for "you" to →"P-O-N-D-E-R"←!!!!!!!
with an (→"O-P-E-N"← door) in the "mind"
rather than (F-O-R →"ever"→ SCREW "UP"←)
like the →"KNOW IT ALLS"← WHO A-L-L-O-W-E-D
the →"S-E-L-F"← force to →"C-L-O-S-E"←!!! "their
minds" placing "them" →"OUT"← side of
Almighty "GOD'S" →"P-R-O-T-E-C-T-I-V-E CUSTODY"← .

JC

October 23rd, 1987

"Archbishop" → Marcel Lefebvre ←

→ "M-I-S-F-O-R-T-U-N-E" is the "E-X-P-R-E-S-S-I-O-N"
held by Almighty "G-O-D" to "DAMN"
for → "A-L-L" Eternity → "THOSE" ← who
incur → "HIS" ← wrath for → "A-L-L-O-W-I-N-G"
the → "S-E-L-F" ← force controlling → "THEM"
through an → "U-N" ← natural → "F-O-R-C-E"
to EN → "D-A-N-G-E-R" ← THE → "lives" ← of
→ "THOSE" ← attempting to "F-I-N-D" their
"WAY" -

"Archbishop" → Marcel · Lefebvre ←

→ "YOU" W-I-L-L !!! encounter → "M-I-S-F-O-R-T-U-NE"
→ "U-N" ← less → "YOU" "S-T-O-P" !!! "blinding"
your "S-E-L-F" (through → "M-O-R-T-A-L" fear)
of taking the → "F-I-N-A-L" step !!! that
→ "W-I-L-L" !!! "cut" the "U-M-B-I-L-I-C-A-L" cord
→ "B-I-N-D-I-N-G" Almighty "GOD" to the

"D-E-S-O-L-A-T-E" debris whose flagrant "S-I-N-S" revolutionized the "D-I-R-E-C-T-I-ON upon "W-H-I-C-H" Jesus Christ "THE" GoD "Man "Set" "HIS" Church "O-N" !!!!!!! ·

"Archbishop" Marcel Lefebvre "L-I-K-E" ! Peter "YOU" "abandon" the "P-A-S-T-O-R-A-L protection "YOU" freely "A-C-C-E-P-T-E-D by "YOUR" refusal !!!!!!! to "step o-u-t" from "U-N-D-E-R" the "P-E-E-R" pressure of "THOSE" who "G-O-V-E-R-N" in the "R-E-M-A-I-N-S" of the "C-H-U-R-C-H that "M-U-S-T" !!! Archbishop Marcel Lefebvre be "C-U-T" !!! away "A-L-L-O-W-I-N-G" them to "P-U-R-S-U-E" their "C-R-U-C-I-F-Y-I-N-G" (IDEOLOGIES) leaving "YOU" Archbishop Marcel Lefebvre the "R-E-M-N-A-N-T" !!! of almighty "GOD'S" Church "S-T-I-L-L" !!!

hanging I-N "D-E-S-P-I-T-E" the "R-E-B-E-L"
prelate "W-H-O" continues to "F-L-I-R-T" !!!
with "M-I-S-F-O-R-T-U-N-E" !!!!!!!
(through "M-O-R-T-A-L" fear) of taking
the "F-I-N-A-L" step that "W-I-L-L" !!!
prevent "MAN" from "CORRUPTING"
the "ENTIRE") Church

November 20th, 1989

Archbishop Marcel Lefebvre

Once upon a "TIME" Life "L-O-O-K-E-D" to those →"HE"← called to "S-E-R-V-E" →"HIS"← purpose in a →very← "S-P-E-C-I-A-L light giving them the "V-E-R-Y" same "opportunity" to accept "O-R" →"reject"← the possibility that their "E-X-I-S-T-S" "ONE" in whom →"N-E-V-E-R"← !!!!!!! →"L-O-O-K-E-D"← beyond the "C-A-P-A-C-I-T-Y" of "MANS" natural tendency to →"R-E-M-A-I-N"← !!!!!!! in →"C-O-N-T-R-O-L"← dispelling "A-N-Y" possibility of comprehending the →"MAKE up"← of the →"FORCE"← !!! responsible for their →"EXISTENCE"

Arbishop Marcel Lefebvre →"W-H-Y"← !!! do →"Y-O-U"← "refuse" !!! to "A-C-K-N-O-W-L-E-D-G-E"

"ONE" who "W-A-S" the instrument responsible for putting to "R-E-S-T" !!! "YOUR" mortal "F-E-A-R" !!!!!!!!!!!! of facing "U-P" to "A-N-Y" !!!!!!!!!!!! situation "T-H-A-T" called on "YOUR" person for "B-O-L-D-N-E-S-S" .

Archbishop Marcel Lefebvre "W-H-Y" !!! do "Y-O-U" "refuse" !!! to "A-C-K-N-O-W-L-E-D-G "ONE" who "W-A-S" the instrument responsible for "A-L-L" !!!!!!!!!!!! the "S-O-L-U-T-I-O-N-S" !!! to "YOUR" !!!!!!! problems !!! .

Archbishop Marcel Lefebvre "W-H-Y" !!!!!!!! do "Y-O-U" "refuse" !!!!!!! to "A-C-K-N-O-W-L-E-D-G-E "ONE" who "W-A-S" !!!!!!! the instrument responsible for "S-C-A-R-I-N-G" "Y-O-U" !!!

into (facing →U-P←) to(→Y-O-U-R←) !!!
responsibilities "W-I-T-H" the "T-H-R-E-A-T" !!!
of →"M-I-S-F-O-R-T-U-N-E"← .

Archbishop →"Marcel Lefebvre"←
→"Like Y-O-U"← there is another within
YOUR fraternity that →"H-A-S"← to
→"this"← !!! point in →"T-I-M-E"← "refused" !!!
to →"R-E-C-O-G-N-I-Z-E"← the "possibility"
that Almighty "GOD" would "S-T-O-O-P"
to →"C-H-O-O-S-E"← "TWO" "Lay" !!! personalities
with →"O-U-T"← →"A-N-Y"← !!!!!!!!!!!!!
(→"P-R-E"← conceived) "I-D-E-A-S"← about
"ONE" responsible !!! for your existence
→"A-L-L"← !!! because →"H-E"← too "relied" on
the "S-E-L-F" !!! force to "R-E-A-C-H"
→"his"← decision ←!!!!!!!!!!!!! for
"refusing" !!! to become →"I-N-V-O-L-V-E-D"←

in "A-N-Y" !!!!!!!! manner with "ONE" of "TWO" instruments responsible in "THEIR" attempt to "O-P-E-N" the _mind_ of "ONE" !!!!!!!! _puffed_ "U-P" "S-E-L-F" _controlled_ !!!!!!!! "A-R-R-O-G-A-N-T" _know it_ "A-L-L" !!! "T-Y-P-E" of individual "W-H-O" !!!!!!!! _believes_ he "H-A-S" !!! "God" altogether "T-H-R-O-U-G-H" letters of which those addressed to his person are "R-E" _copied_ & herewith enclosed for Y-O-U to "P-O-N-D-E-R"

Archbishop Marcel Lefebvre
Almighty "GOD" "N-E-V-E-R" !!!!!!!!!!!!! _reneges_ on a "P-R-O-M-I-S-E" should "Y-O-U" Marcel Truly "B-E-L-I-E-V-E" !!! the "L-E-T-T-E-R" in which the "DOOR" to _Almighty_ "GOD'S" Kingdom "H-A-S" !!!

been →*O-P-E-N-E-D*← for *Y-O-U*
then "*S-U-R-E-L-Y*" marcel it becomes
a matter of →*S-I-M-P-L-E*← _logic_ to
"*PRE*" _suppose_ that "*Y-O-U*" *must*
"*G-I-V-E*" similar →*C-R-E-D-E-N-C-E*← to
A-L-L of the →*O-T-H-E-R*← _letters_
that "*Y-O-U*" received as they *A-L-L*
originate from the *P-E-N* of
the "*V-E-R-Y*" _same_ *I-N-S-T-R-U-M-E-N-T* !!!

Enos 3.

c.c.l. "*BISHOP*" Richard Williamson

Archbishop Marcel Lefebvre

To "L-O-O-K" on Almighty "GOD" as a "FORCE" without "DIMENSION" without "SUBSTANCE" without a "TRINITARION make up "contradicts" the "A-P-O-S-T-O-L-I-C" "belief" held by those "responsible" for "U-N" raveling the "M-A-K-E" up "given" Almighty "GOD" which came to pass following the (→"B-I-R-T-H" of CHRISTIANITY←) bringing a ("N-E-W" dimension) to the "AGE old" concept of mans "C-R-E-A-T-O-R" held by these "responsible" for the "R-E" generation of "ALL" mankind through "ONE" called "Abraham" "WHO" relied on the "D-E-E-P" & "I-N" comprehensible "N-A-T-U-R-E" of Almighty "GOD" to manifest "H-I-S" Spirit

through whatever means He deems
"fit" to get "HIS" message across enabling
Abraham to receive the "E-V-E-R-L-A-S-T-I-N-G"
word from Almighty "GOD" that "H-I-S"
stock would "N-E-V-E-R" become
"O-R-P-H-A-N-S" in "R-E-T-U-R-N" for "HANGING in
making it possible for MANS Creator
to come in to this W-O-R-L-D as a
member of the ("J-E-W" ish) stock to
"S-E-T" in motion "His" PLAN for
assuring the "C-O-V-E-N-A-N-T" made to
Abraham by Almighty "GOD" that His
message of "S-A-L-V-A-T-I-O-N" for the
"J-E-W-S" would be (kept "S-A-F-E") for
them in S-P-I-T-E of "A-L-L" the "PAIN"
"SUFFERING" "HUMILIATION" & "REJECTION"
"He" "FORE" knew would befall "ONE"
whose "E-A-R-T-H-L-Y" existence gave

Almighty "GOD" a-W-A-Y to

make-"FELT" "HIS" _presence_ in a

"H-U-M-A-N" _way_ in order that "HE"

could "EXPERIENCE" (as→man←)

the temptations & sufferings to

whatever degree ???????

"W-I-T-H-O-U-T" benifit of "P-O-S-I-T-I-O-N"

_JC_

November 23 rd, 1987.

Cardinal Edoward Gagnon

To →"S-I-T"← in "JUDGEMENT"→"like"←Pontius Pilate "O-V-E-R" the "B-O-D-Y" still standing "T-H-A-T" →"belongs"← to Almighty "G-O-D" "M-U-S-T" in →"like"← fashion →"A-C-C-E-P-T"← the "P-E-N-A-L-T-Y" incurred for →"A-N-Y"←!! action having an "A-D-V-E-R-S-E" effect on the →"O-N-L-Y"←!!! remnant of the →"T-R-U-E"←!!! Roman Catholic Church founded by Jesus Christ on Peter still hanging in →"D-E-S-P-I-T-E"←!!! the "P-L-O-Y-S" of →"T-H-O-S-E"← within the →"I-N-N-E-R"← Sanctum of the "U-N-I-V-E-R-S-A-L" Church →"W-H-O"← have "S-U-R-R-E-P-T-I-T-I-O-U-S-L-Y" conspired to →"U-N-D-O"← the →"O-N-E"← & →"only"←"T-E-M-P-L-E" containing !!!!!!! Almighty "GOD".

<u>Cardinal Edward Gagnon</u>

→ "<u>Like</u>" ← Pontius Pilate "<u>y-o-u</u>" → <u>now</u> ←

"<u>S-T-A-N-D</u>" → "<u>vis à vis</u>" ← with "ONE"

who → "<u>F-R-E-E-L-Y</u>" ← <u>dropped</u> "HIS" → <u>guard</u>

through → "<u>L-O-Y-A-L-T-Y</u>" ← to "ONE"

who "HE" desperately → <u>W-A-N-T-E-D</u> → to

"<u>BELIEVE</u>" in which <u>has</u> "<u>N-O-W</u>" !!!

"Cardinal" <u>Edward Gagnon</u> as a

"<u>R-E-S-U-L-T</u>" of "<u>YOUR</u>" <u>involvement</u> !!!

→ "<u>like</u>" ← Pontius Pilate <u>placed "y-o-u"</u> !!!

between a → "<u>R-O-C-K</u>" ← & a → "<u>H-A-R-D-P-L-A-C-E</u>"

"Cardinal" <u>Edward Gagnon</u>

→ "<u>Like</u>" ← Christ "<u>you</u>" → "<u>cannot</u>" ← !!!!!

→ "<u>E-S-C-A-P-E</u>" ← the "<u>O-U-T</u>"come of the

"<u>task</u>" → "you" → ← "<u>F-R-E-E-L-Y</u>" !!!!!!!!!!!! <u>accepted</u> .

JG

February 25th, 1982

"CARDINAL" Joseph Ratzinger

THIS "LETTER" COMES from "TWO" STRANGERS" WHO
ARE BEING "COMPELLED" TO WARN "YOU" OF
the "SPIRITUAL DANGER" SURROUNDING "ONE"
WHO BELIEVES in "DESTROYING" "ALL" TRADITIONAL
BELIEFS GIVEN the "Roman Catholic Church" by
"Jesus Christ."

"CARDINAL" Joseph Ratzinger the "HOUR" is "NEAR"
BRINGING to "ONE" WHO "DELIBERATELY" CONSPIRED
to bring about the "DOWNFALL" of "ONE" THAT
"UPHELD" YOUR "HERETICAL" ACTIONS AT A "TIME" in
which "you" "CARDINAL" Ratzinger WERE "USING" YOUR
"POWER" & INFLUENCE WITH "RECKLESS" ABANDON MISFORTUNE

"CARDINAL" Ratzinger their is "ONE" WHO "SHARED"

SIMILAR BELIEFS HELPING "US" IN OUR ATTEMPTS TO "DESTROY" THE TRADITIONAL BELIEFS OF THE CHURCH THAT WERE "STAUNCHLY" SAFEGUARDED BY THOSE WHOM "WILL" NOW "BE" OPEN TO AN "INDEFENSIBLE" ATTACK BY "ONE" WHO CONSPIRED TO PENETRATE THE "RANKS" OF THOSE GIVEN the RESPONSIBILITY of SAFEGUARDING the "TRADITIONAL LAWS" of "GOD'S" Church

"CARDINAL" Ratzinger the "HOUR" is "NEAR" BRINGING to "ONE" WHO BELIEVES in "DESTROYING" the BELIEFS HELD BY MANY CONFUSED CHRISTIANS TO BE THE ONLY WAY in which "THEY" can FIND "SALVATION" the "KNOWLEDGE" to HELP "US" to "REVERSE" the "PATH" WE HAVE CHOSEN MAKING IT POSSIBLE for "YOU" "CARDINAL" Joseph Ratzinger to "FIND" SPIRITUAL SAFETY.

The "MESSAGE" contained "HERE IN" CLEARLY "FORETELLS" "ALL" "CARDINAL" Ratzinger THAT "WILL" COME TO PASS

should "you" _FAIL_ to HEED the "_WORDS_" of "TWO" STRANGERS.

October 28th, 1985.

Cardinal Joseph Ratzinger

To "F-O-R-G-E" a "L-I-N-K" that "WILL" give "y-o-u" the wherewithal to "F-E-N-D" against "ALL" those "ecclesiastics" ("W-H-O" take) (→"A-N-Y"← part) Joseph in the ("A-P-P-R-O-A-C-H-I-N-G" storm) which "W-I-L-L" (→"ROB"←) !!!!! the "BODY" responsible for "S-A-F-E" guarding→ ??? the "R-E-M-A-I-N-S" of Roman Catholic "D-O-C-T-R-I-N-E"→OPEN"← !!! to "A-T-T-A-C-K" should→"y-o-u"← fail to "A-G-A-I-N" !!! "HEED" the "WORDS" of "TWO" strangers ("WHO" are) being moved by "ONE" to "TELL"→you← that "U-N-L-E-S-S" the "ONE" who "D-R-E-S-S-E-S" him→"S-E-L-F"← !!! as the →"FISHER"← of men "S-T-O-P-S" the →"V-E-N-D-E-T-T-A"← !!!!!!!!!!!! between→"TWO"←

(→"O-P-P-O-S-I-N-G"← !!!!!!!! "factions") "L-O-C-K-E-D"
in a →"P-O-W-E-R"← struggle)→"F-U-E-L-E-D"← !!!!
by "ONE" who →"H-A-T-E-S"← !!! "you"
Joseph for the "M-A-N-N-E-R" in which
"you" come to "G-R-A-S-P" with "T-O-P-I-C-S"
concerning "Y-O-U-R" !!! religious →"I-N-S-I-G-H-T"←
that →"H-A-S"← ("set" the "S-T-A-G-E") for the
(→"final"← !!!!!!!!!!!!! "ACT") which →"W-I-L-L"←
determine the →"F-A-T-E"← Cardinal Joseph
Ratzinger of →"ONE"← who →"D-E-A-L-S"← in
"conspiracy" →"PROVIDED"← !!!!!!! "you" →"listen"←
to "TWO" Strangers who "HAVE" ("accepted")
a "C-A-L-L-I-N-G" wherein ("THEY" believe) !!!
Almighty "GOD" →"I-S"← using "THEM" to
→"S-I-G-N-A-L"← !!! the "M-A-N-N-E-R" in which
→"GOD"← intends to "WRAP-up" !!!!!!!!!!!! the
"F-I-N-A-L Chapter" of →"MANS"← infidelity to
his →"CREATOR"← by →"O-N-C-E"← again →"S-H-A-R-I-N-G"←

(→"H-U-M-A-N"← form) !!!!!!!!!!!!!! that Joseph Almighty "GOD" →HAS← taken as →"HIS"← !!! →VERY own← vehicles Giving "HIM" the (→"I-D-E-N-T-I-C-A-L"← Route) →"HE"← Chose to (→"MAKE"← felt) "HIS" presence in the (→"F-L-E-S-H"← !!!) of →"ONE"← called Jesus Christ "WHO" differed from Almighty "GOD'S" →"TWO"← Witnesses in that →"HE"← was →"P-U-T"← to →"D-E-A-T-H"← by a →"HARD"← corrupt →"CORE"← of "R-E-L-I-G-I-O-U-S" zealots "WHO" refused to (→"listen"→O-R←→"believe"←) that any hardships "W-O-U-L-D" come upon them for THEIR →"S-E-L-F"← induced "ACT" which "WAS" condemned by the "CHRISTIAN"??? GENTILE whose "R-E-L-I-G-I-O-U-S" beliefs TAKE on whatever "VIEW" point is →"DEEMED"← to find "F-A-V-O-U-R" with the →"B-O-D-Y"← currently "D-I-C-T-A-T-I-N-G"

OR →"B-E-H-A-L-F"← of Almighty "GOD"
WHO "is"← being →"U-S-E-D"← !!! by a
"C-O-L-L-E-C-T-I-V-E" body of →"S-E-L-F" righteous
"P-R-E-L-A-T-E-S" who →MAKE← up the
→"N-U-C-L-E-U-S"← of what →"HAS"← become
the "W-O-R-L-D'S" →largest← religious
"BODY" founded by "ONE" who "SAID"
that →"HE"← would →"R-E-T-U-R-N"←
Cardinal Joseph Ratzinger →N-O-T← as
a "TYPE" of →"WISHY-WASHY"← individual
→"A-N-Y← one" can →"F-I-N-D"← forgiveness
with →"B-U-T"← as Scripture (T-E-L-L-S "US")
→"I-N"← the →"F-O-R-M-S"← of →"HIS"← "TWO" (Witnesses)
that →"H-A-V-E"← Joseph been →"U-S-E-D"←
by "GOD" to →"assist" "chastise" "warn"← &
→"C-O-N-D-E-M-N"← "SELECT" individuals
both ("IN" & "outside") of God's Church
for THEIR Personal (→"S-C-R-E-w" up←)

of Almighty "GOD'S" "PLAN" for mankind
Giving to →"S-O-M-E"← of "YOU" the
opportunity to "M-E-N-D" your "WAYS"
rather than continue on a →"J-O-U-R-N-E-Y"←
headed for→"H-E-L-L"←.

Cardinal Joseph Ratzinger As "CUSTODIAN"
in Charge of the Office→"R-E-S-P-O-N-S-I-B-L-E"
for→"S-A-F-E"← guarding the "D-O-C-T-R-I-N-A-L"
→"remains"←!!! of a "CHURCH" under→"C-O-N-S-T-A-N-T"
attack) by a →"HARD"←"corrupt"→"CORE"←
of "R-E-L-I-G-I-O-U-S" Zealots→"H-E-A-D-E-D"←
by "ONE"→intent← on rendering
(→"it"← I-M-P-O-T-E-N-T) is "CAUSE" for "TWO"
being "MOVED" to "ENCLOSE" a copy of a
letter "S-E-N-T" to "ONE" who (has→"N-O-T"←)!!!
"C-H-A-N-G-E-D"→his"←(→"L-I-F-E"← style) .

6

May "Y-O-U" Cardinal Joseph Ratzinger "VIEW" this letter with an →"O-P-E-N"← mind rather than "L-O-O-K" on it as coming from "TWO" whose →"M-I-N-D-S"← are →"still circling"← for a "LANDING" the "B-E-N-E-F-I-T-S" to "YOU" Joseph will be of a →"K-I-N-D"← "THAT" will "O-V-E-R come "YOUR" present "PLIGHT".

April 5th 1986.

"Cardinal" Joseph Ratzinger

→"L-I-F-E"← is "FULL" of →"S-U-R-P-R-I-S-E-S"← that provide →"S-O-M-E"← of "U-S" the opportunity to "ACCEPT" or "REJECT" the "TRADITIONAL" views we hang on to which tend to influence →our← "B-E-H-A-V-I-O-U-R" causing "THOSE" who →"A-C-T"← in this "fashion" to "M-I-S-S" the →"T-A-R-G-E-T"← "Life" !!! "HAS" created for "E-A-C-H" according to (→"HIS" or "HER"← P-U-R-P-O-S-E) in "Lifes" PLAN to "B-R-I-N-G" together for "HIS" final →"P-U-S-H"← against →"A-L-L"← who →"E-V-E-R"← (fell →"S-H-O-R-T"←) of "T-H-E-I-R" target "S-O-L-E-Y" because they HAD "Cardinal" Joseph Ratzinger →"B-O-X-E-D"← "Almighty "GOD"

in →"R-E-F-U-S-I-N-G"← !!! to "A-C-K-N-O-W-L-E-D-G-E"
that God "W-O-U-L-D" (→"S-T-O-O-P"←) to
("bring "A-B-O-U-T") the "D-O-W-N-F-A-L-L" of "ONE"
that was →"A-S-K-E-D"← !!!!!!!! by "Almighty" "GOD"
to "B-R-I-N-G" →"HIS"← !!! Church back
to its "T-R-A-D-I-T-I-O-N-A-L" "COURSE" in
"TIME" by means of (→"THREE"← letters)
"Cardinal" Joseph Ratzinger →"P-L-A-C-E-D"←
in the "mind" of "ONE" of the
"TWO" individuals that were also
called upon to →"MAKE"← the →"S-A-M-E"←
decision to "ACCEPT" or "R-E-J-E-C-T" the
possibility !!!!!!!!!!!! "T-H-A-T" "Almighty" "GOD"
"C-R-E-A-T-O-R" with "O-U-T" !!!!!!!!!!!!!!
dimension ("W-O-U-L-D" "S-T-O-O-P")
to →"U-S-E"← some "UNK-N-O-W-N"
un"S-O-P-H-I-S-T-I-C-A-T-E-D" "human" FORMS
is cause for "anyone" to CHANGE

what→"EVER"← preconceived "I-D-E-A-S"
they HAVE about <u>Almighty</u> "GOD'S"
→"MODUS OPERANDI"← !!! .

"Cardinal" Joseph Ratzinger when
("W-E"→<u>have</u>←) !!!!!!!!!!! an "I-N-F-L-A-T-E-D"
opinion of "O-U-R" God→"G-I-V-E-N"← intelligen
to "D-I-S-C-E-R-N" the <u>S-piritual→"P-U-L-S-E"←</u>
of <u>Almighty</u> "GOD"→"<u>S-T-I-R-R-I-N-G</u>"← the
→"<u>A-D-R-E-N-A-L-I-N-E</u>"← in "U-S" to "<u>WHAT</u>"→ever←
→"L-E-V-E-L"← of →<u>"ANGER"</u>← "WE" reach in
→"P-R-E"← <u>judging</u> without possessing
sufficient "in"→S-I-G-H-T← into the
"M-I-N-D-S" of <u>T-H-O-S-E</u> →"WE" <u>really</u>←
(<u>do</u>→"N-O-T"← <u>know</u>) !!!!!!! .

"Cardinal" Joseph Ratzinger→"<u>S-T-U-P-I-D-I-T-Y</u>"←
is a "<u>W-O-R-D</u>" held to→"<u>L-A-B-E-L</u>"←

"A-N-Y" individual that fails to measure "U-P" to "S-O-C-I-E-T-I-E-S" criterion on matters that "R-E-V-E-A-L" the "C-R-A-C-K-S" in "our" "I-N-T-E-L-L-E-C-T" should "S-T-O-O-P" in "ORDER" to "ascertain" the real purpose for going on the "D-E-F-E-N-S-I-V-E" rather than direct our "A-C-T-I-V-I-T-I-E-S" in the "U-S-U-A-L" way taking advantage of "E-V-E-R-Y" opportunity "W-E" believe will "K-E-EP" "U-S" on the "R-I-G-H-T" side of "L-I-F-E" is being "G-I-V-E-N" "T-H-R-E-E" copies of letters to "O-N-E" who was "also" of the "O-P-I-N-I-O-N" that the "ONE" whom "E-X-P-R-E-S-S-E-D" "HIS" thoughts "S-O" forcefully to "one" in charge of "GOD'S" church "M-U-S-T" be "I-R-R-A-T-I-O-N-A-L" !!!!!!! •

5

"Cardinal" Joseph Ratzinger "A-F-T-E-R" reading →"T-H-I-S"← letter together with "A-L-L" attached "C-O-P-I-E-S" including →"ONE"← which was →"D-I-R-E-C-T-E-D"← to the →"O-N-L-Y"← remaining →"S-U-R-V-I-V-O-R"← possessing information →"R-E-L-E-V-A-N-T"← to "HER" purpose for being "K-E-P-T" to →"FULFILL"← the "R-O-L-E" "Life" assigned !!! "HER" which is being "circumvented" by →"ONE"← who is →"M-U-Z-Z-L-I-N-G"← a "most" susceptible "T-O-O-L" to →"P-R-E-V-E-N-T"← !!!!!!!!!!!! the "UN-"M-A-S-K-I-N-G" of →"T-H-O-S-E"← "Cardinal" Joseph Ratzinger who →"Life"← is "P-O-I-N-T-I-N-G" an →"A-N-G-R-Y"← finger "A-T" →"is"← in the "M-I-N-D" of this (→"U-N-S-O-P-H-I-S-T-I-G-A-T-E-D"← individual) →"N-O-T"← thinking "R-A-T-I-O-N-A-L-L-Y"

as are "ANY" "Cardinal" Joseph Ratzinger
who E-I-T-H-E-R →"view"← them-S-E-L-V-E-S"!!
or "HAVE" been "L-A-B-E-L-E-D" by "S-O-C-I-E-T-Y"
as being "I-N-T-E-L-L-E-C-T-U-A-L-L-Y" endowed
(should→"R-E-A-L-L-Y"←) "Cardinal" Joseph
Ratzinger→"S-T-O-O-P"← to the→"L-E-V-E-L"
of the un"S-O-P-H-I-S-T-I-C-A-T-E-D"
(who "V-I-E-W"→"Life"←) with (an→"O-P-E-N"→mind
rather than→"S-T-U-P-I-D-L-Y"← attempt
to→"B-O-X"← Almighty "GOD"→"I-N"←!!!

JC

October 31st, 1988.

→ "Bishop" → Richard Williamson

→ N-O-T-W-I-T-H-S-T-A-N-D-I-N-G → ones shortsightedness
"OUR" religeous "S-T-A-T-E" dictates the
manner in which "WE" come to
"G-R-A-S-P" with the → I-N-E-X-P-L-I-C-A-B-L-E → !!!
that → blinds → "U-S" with a "D-E-E-P" &
"F-O-R-E-B-O-D-I-N-G" feeling of "ONE" who
does "N-O-T" intend to (→ "S-T-E-P" out →)
from "U-N-D-E-R" the "Spiritual influence"
(→ "S-U-R-R-O-U-N-D-I-N-G → him) to ascertain
the outlandish "P-U-R-P-O-S-E" behind
the "A-C-T-I-O-N-S" of "TWO" extreme → L-A-Y → !!!
personalities whose → M-O-D-U-S O-P-E-R-A-N-D-I →
suggest a → C-O-U-P-L-E → who → A-R-E → !!!!!!!
→ N-O-N → composmentis".

2

"B-I-S-H-O-P" Richard Williamson "W-H-Y"!!! does "Life" "R-E-F-L-E-C-T"!!!!!!!! "His" "F-O-R-M" in a "H-U-M-A-N" way ???

"B-I-S-H-O-P" Richard Williamson "W-H-Y"!! did "Jesus" "R-E-F-L-E-C-T"!!!!!!!! "His" "D-I-V-I-N-I-T-Y" in a "H-U-M-A-N" way ???

"B-I-S-H-O-P" Richard Williamson "W-H-Y"!!! has "M-A-N" "failed"!!!!!!!!!!!! in his "S-E-A-R-C-H" to ("find" "R-E-V-E-A-L-E-D" truth)!

"B-I-S-H-O-P" Richard Williamson "S-C-R-I-P-T-U-R-E" tells "T-H-O-S-E" seeking "K-N-O-W-L-E-D-G-E" ("that") which "S-E-L-F" will "A-C-C-E-P-T" rather than ("T-R-U-T-H") simply "S-T-A-T-E-D".

3

→"B-I-S-H-O-P"← Richard Williamson →N-O-T-H-I-N-G"← !! can →"C-O-M-E"← to →"P-A-S-S"← →"un-T-I-L" →"S-O-M-E" body →"decides"← on a "course" of →"A-C-T-I-O-N"← .

→"B-I-S-H-O-P"← Richard Williamson →"N-O-T-H-I-N-G" →"W-I-L-L"← !!! come to →"P-A-S-S"← →"un-L-E-S-S →"we"← →"S-T-O-P"← !!! fashioning Almighty "GOD" to →"F-I-T"← into some →"K-I-N-D"← ??? of "M-O-L-D acceptable !!! to "OUR" religious "S-T-A-T-E & →"L-O-O-K"← !!! with an →"O-P-E-N"← door !!! in →"YOUR"← mind Richard →"D-I-S-P-E-L-L-I-N-G"← these →"P-R-E"← conceived "I-D-E-A-S" concerning the (→"M-O-D-U-S OPERANDI"←) of Almighty "GOD" that keep "U-S" from →"E-V-E-R"← !!!!!!! comprehending the W-H-Y's !!!!!!!!!!!! in "GOD'S"→ make "U-P"← Richard Williamson

4

→"I-S"← !!! that "you" & "your" "ilk" !!! →"N-E-V-E-R"← !!!
give →"U-P"← the →"S-E-L-F"← force responsible !!!
for keeping →"U-S"← in a →"C-O-N-F-U-S-E-D"←
condition that →"H-A-S"← !!! become the
→"R-O-O-T"← responsible for bringing
the →"S-O-L-E"← remnant of "God's" Church
to the →"B-R-I-N-K"← !!! of destruction
endangering the "F-A-I-T-H" →filled← "F-L-O-C-K"
→"W-H-O"← !!! were at a "L-O-S-S" to comprehend
the "W-H-Y's" !!! behind the →"A-C-T-I-O-N-S"←
of →"the"← "P-R-E-L-A-T-E" who →"A-C-C-E-P-T-E-D"←
the →"M-A-N-T-L-E"← of "responsibility" to
→"C-H-O-O-S-E"← without →"B-E-N-I-F-I-T"← the
→"O-N-L-Y"← path that "W-I-L-L" provide
"H-U-M-A-N-I-T-Y" a →"way"← to come to
→"G-R-A-S-P"← the →"significance"← of "A-C-C-E-P-T-I-N-G"
as →"G-O-S-P-E-L"← the "outlandish purpose !!!

behind the "A-C-T-I-O-N-S" of "TWO" extreme "L-A-Y" !!! personalities→"W-H-O-S-E" soul !!!→"A-I-M" is to→"W-R-A-P" up !!! "THEIR" obligation to "ONE" who→"I-S" !!! giving "THEM" to→"S-E-N-S-E" the "futility" !!!!!!! of bringing about→"A-N-Y" !!!!!!!→"change" in a→"B-U-N-C-H" of→"S-T-I-F-F N-E-C-K-E-D" !!! "ecclesiastics" "T-H-A-T" "will" "W-I-N-D up" "committing" !!! the "V-E-R-Y" !!! same "C-R-I-M-E" "THEIR" "Jewish" "C-O-U-N-T-E-R-P-A-R-T-S" "have" "R-E-F-U-S-E-D" to→"A-C-C-E-P-T" ("because") !!! THEY "also" "B-I-S-H-O-P" !!! Richard Williamson fashioned Almighty "GOD" to→"F-I-T" !!! into their "S-E-L-F" !!! conceived "M-O-L-D" "closing" the "D-O-O-R" to→"A-N-Y" !!! possibility that "mans" "CREATOR" alone "FASHIONS" "Himself" !!!!!!!!!!!!! in the "very same"

"F-O-R-M" given →"man"← using →"His"← !!!
→"P-O-W-E-R"← of →"P-O-S-I-T-I-O-N"← !!!!!!!!!!!!
to "O-P-E-R-A-T-E" in →"A-N-Y"← !!!!!!!! "manner"
→"HE"← !!! decrees →"F-I-T"← "permitting" →"ALL"← !!!
→"B-I-S-H-O-P"← Richard Williamson a
→"W-I-L-L"← "free" !!! to →"C-H-O-O-S-E"← !!! the →"WAY"←
of the "Jew" by →"C-L-O-S-I-N-G"← !!! the "D-O-O-R"
in →"YOUR"← !!! mind .

Encs. 4

PACKET #2.

January 2nd, 2008

Jacob Neusner

In "OUR" endless "Q-U-E-S-T" for understanding "WE" set about by "L-O-O-K-I-N-G" for "CLUES" that "W-I-L-L" provide "U-S" with the "A-N-S-W-E-R-S" that ("S-E-L-F" "WILL accept") rather than "FACE" "F-A-C-T-S" that "C-L-E-A-R-L-Y" "DEMONSTRATES" "OUR" ("LACK" of "WILLINGNESS") to let "G-O" of "A-L-L" "WE" have been "T-A-U-G-H-T" to "B-E-L-I-E-V-E" making this "T-A-S-K" "ONE" in which "Y-O-U" "Jacob Neusner" "MUST" cast aside "Y-O-U-R" ("know it A-L-L")??? religious "BELIEFS" & "L-O-O-K" "W-I-T-H" an ("O-P-E-N" DOOR) in the "MIND" that "W-I-L-L" "GIVE" Jacob the "O-N-L-Y" "WAY" to come to "GRIPS" with "R-E-A-L-I-T-Y" "I-S" for Jacob to "L-O-O-K" ON this L-I-F-E as a G-I-A-N-T "B-A-L-L-P-A-R-K" "WITH" "THREE" "P-L-A-Y-E-R-S"

"C-A-L-L-E-D"

THE "F-O-R-C-E" OF "G-O-O-D" THE "F-O-R-C-E" OF "E-V-I-L"
(THE "F-O-R-C-E" OF "S-E-L-F")

Jacob Neusner in "OUR" "E-N-D" less "Q-U-E-S-T"
for "T-R-U-T-H" "WE" put into "PRACTICE"
THE "F-O-R-C-E" "C-A-L-L-E-D" "S-E-L-F"
To "C-O-P-E" with "A-N-Y" "C-O-N-C-E-I-V-A-B-L-E"
"PREDICAMENT" "WE" are "C-O-N-F-R-O-N-T-E-D"
"WITH" (G-I-V-I-N-G "U-S") the "W-H-E-R-E-W-I-T-H-A-L"
to "MAKE" the "C-A-L-L" "W-E" "THINK"?
to be "R-I-G-H-T" without "E-V-E-R" taking
the "T-I-M-E" to "S-T-O-P" & "L-O-O-K"
at the "T-W-O" "other" "P-L-A-Y-E-R-S"
"W-H-O" "ARE" ALSO "A-T-T-E-M-P-T-I-N-G"!!
TO "C-O-N-T-R-O-L" the "F-O-R-C-E" called
"S-E-L-F" to "A-C-H-I-E-V-E" "THEIR" "P-U-R-P-O-S-E"
"H-E-R-E" "LEAVING" Jacob Neusner

a "W-I-L-L" "FREE" to "CHOOSE" "H-I-S" "DESTINY" together "WITH" "A-L-L" "JEWS" "BY" "C-L-O-S-I-N-G" the "D-O-O-R" in the "M-I-N-D" to "A-L-L" that "H-I-S" "CONSCIENCE" & "GOD" "G-I-V-E-N" "Common Sense" "H-A-V-E" been making "H-I-M" aware of.

Jacob Neusner

May "Y-O-U" "L-O-O-K" on this "L-E-T-T-E-R" as coming from "ONE" "W-H-O" is "ASKING" Jacob to "P-O-N-D-E-R" "carefully" "A-L-L" "T-H-O-U-G-H-T-S" "GIVEN" "Y-O-U" as to their "S-O-U-R-C-E" "making" it "P-O-S-S-I-B-L-E" for "Y-O-U" Jacob to "FIND" the "S-O-L-U-T-I-O-N" that "W-I-L-L" !!! "GIVE" "Y-O-U" the "S-T-R-E-N-G-T-H" to "L-O-O-K" to the "F-O-R-C-E" "Called" "G-O-O-D" for "A-L-L" "YOUR" "N-E-E-D-S" "R-E-L-Y-I-N-G"

ON "H-I-M" to "GIVE" "Y-O-U" Jacob Neusner
the "O-N-L-Y" !!! "WAY" to "F-I-N-D" "SALVATION"
together "WITH" "Y-O-U-R" "PEOPLE" the "J-E-W-S"

Jacob Neusner

In "O-U-R" "E-N-D" less "Q-U-E-S-T" for "P-R-O-O-F"
"W-E" "BECOME" "O-B-S-E-S-S-E-D" with the "D-A-T-A"
"WE" have "U-N" covered through "YEARS"
of Re "S-E-A-R-C-H" making the "T-A-S-K"
of coming to "GRIPS" with what
"WE" are "N-O-W" being "P-R-E-S-E-N-T-E-D" WITH
leaves "U-S" in a (very "D-E-E-P" dilemma)
with "very little" "M-I-N-D" "manouvering
room" therefore the "F-O-R-C-E" called "G-O-O-D"
that "Y-O-U" are "N-O-W" being "MOVED"
to "L-O-O-K" to "is" enclosing "additional
"D-A-T-A" in the "FORM" of "L-E-T-T-E-R-S"

5

"G-I-V-E-N" "TWO" "LAY" personalities "THAT" were "A-T-T-E-M-P-T-I-N-G" to "COMPREHEND" the "M-I-N-D" "BOGGLING" "COMPLEXITIES" of "THIS" "F-O-R-G-E" "THAT" "L-O-O-K-E-D" ON "T-W-O" OF "H-I-S" "WAYWARD" "Children" "S-E-E-K-I-N-G" to "F-I-N-D" the "REAL" meaning for "O-U-R" existence "H-E-R-E" enabling "H-I-M" to "COMMUNICATE" through the ("O-P-E-N" DOOR) !!!!!!! in "THEIR" "M-I-N-D" to "R-E-C-L-A-I-M" "TWO" "S-O-U-L-S" that "H-E" "HAS" "T-A-K-E-N" "as" ("HIS VERY O-W-N" !!!

May 13.th, 2007

Inez

"Almighty God" → "HAS" ← chosen → "Y-O-U" ←
as the "INSTRUMENT" that → "W-I-L-L" ←
be used to prepare the → "F-O-U-N-D-A-T-I-O-N"
upon which the GOD/MAN
Jesus Christ "W-I-L-L" make known
to a "J-E-W"??? the → "MYSTERY" ← surrounding
the → "PERSON" ← named "Jesus".

→ "Almighty "GOD" ← "W-I-L-L" take whatever
steps are required to keep → "H-I-S" ←
→ "T-W-O" ← Witnesses in a → "HEALTHY STATE" ←
to ensure that God's promised
→ "WORD" ← to Abraham be → "F-U-L-L-F-I-L-L-E-D" ←

January 20th, 2006

John & Inez

Almighty "God" Has "R-E-A-C-H-E-D" that POINT in "T-I-M-E" where in THE "S-O-N" OF MAN Jesus Christ "W-I-L-L" return in the "F-L-E-S-H" using the "F-O-R-M-S" of "ALMIGHTY" G-O-D'S ("T-W-O" "Most Loved" P-U-T-T P-U-T-T'S thus making it "P-O-S-S-I-B-L-E" for "H-I-M" to "W-R-A-P up" an OBLIGATION "H-E" made giving to the JEW their WAY to "R-E-P-E-N-T" by way of "A-T-O-N-E-M-E-N-T" exemplifying the "M-A-N-N-E-R" HELD to be the "O-N-L-Y" way Almighty G-O-D "WILL" "F-O-R-G-I-V-E" "THEM" for their "M-I-S-D-E-E-D-S" to "O-N-E" called "Jesus Christ".

Inez:John like Jesus you tend to become →"O-V-E-R-W-R-O-U-G-H-T"← when given a →"S-P-I-R-I-T" ual →"J-O-L-T" making the overall →"T-A-S-K" one in which "Y-O-U" →both← like Jesus "must" "O-V-E-R-C-O-M-E"

John:Inez _almighty_ "God" Has →"R-E-A-C-H-E-D"← that POINT in →"T-I-M-E" where-in →"HE" "will" M-A-K-E" _Known_ to the →"Jews" _using_ the→"F-O-R-M-S" of →"Almighty" ← →"G-O-D-S" (→"T-W-O" _(Witnesses)_) to →"U-N" "ravel" the →"M-Y-S-T-E-R-Y" surrounding the "PERSON" named →"J-E-S-U-S" who became the →"T-A-R-G-E-T" of→"MANS inhumanity to MAN" for→"N-O-T" _succumbing_ to the _demoralizing_ →"P-L-O-Y-S" of a →"B-U-N-C-H" of →"G-O-D-L-E-S-S"→"miscreants"←

"W-H-O" →epitomize← the "M-A-S-S-E-S" that "T-R-A-V-E-R-S-E" TIME clothed in "S-E-L-F" righteousness.

Inez John "History" →TELLS "U-S"← how to "F-O-R-E-tell" the "F-U-T-U-R-E" giving→"U-S" to "S-E-E" the "H-O-P-E-L-E-S-S-N-E-S-S" of bringing→"A-B-O-U-T"← →any← "C-H-A-N-G-E" in "A-L-L" "HUMANITY" that →"HAVE"← allowed the "S-E-L-F" force to remain in →C-O-N-T-R-O-L← .

September 21st, 1987.

John & Inez

To → "C-O-N-T-I-N-U-E" doing "T-H-A-T" which "YOU" both → "B-E-L-I-E-V-E" to be "Life's" "R-O-L-E" for "TWO" → un ← "U-S-U-A-L", → un ← "K-N-O-W-N" → un ← "S-O-P-H-I-S-T-I-C-A-T-E-D" & → un ← "A-F-F-E-C-T-E-D" by the "C-O-U-R-S-E" which was "S-E-T" to → "P-R-E-P-A-R-E" ← "them" for a → "F-E-A-T" that "W-I-L-L" in → "V-O-L-V-E" "placing" (→ "YOUR" → "absolute" ← "T-R-U-S-T" ←) !!!!!!! in the "ONE" invisible → "FORCE" ← known as "LIFE" who "HAS" both → "N-U-R-T-U-R-E-D" ← & → kept ← "S-A-F-E" "HIS" "TWO" chosen by almighty "GOD" to "C-A-R-R-Y" out "A-L-L" that → "W-I-L-L" ← be required of "THEM" from an "I-N-V-I-S-I-B-L-E" force keeping "TWO" struggling to (→ "S-T-A-Y" ← afloat)

in a (→"S-T-A-T-E"← of →"M-E-N-T-A-L"← turmoil from which (→"THEY"← can) !!!!!!!!!!!! →O-V-E-R← come by →W-A-Y← of complete "T-R-U-S-T" in almighty "GOD" "WHO" !!! "L-O-O-K-E-D" on "TWO" of "His" →"W-A-Y"← ward "children" seeking to ("G-A-I-N" some in "S-I-G-H-T") as to "WHAT" !!! this →"L-I-F-E"← was all "A-B-O-U-T" as "THEIR" →Spiritual← "A-P-P-E-T-I-T-E" was found to be "W-A-N-T-I-N-G" beyond the →"S-C-O-P-E"← of →"A-N-Y"← human intelligence to →"S-A-T-I-S-F-Y"← "thus" →"A-R-O-U-S-I-N-G"← a "force" within THEM" that →W-A-N-T-E-D← !!!!!!! to →"R-E"← claim →"TWO"← Souls →"C-A-P-A-B-L-E"← of "surrendering" them →"S-E-L-V-E-S"← in Body Mind & Spirit to "ONE" who "H-A-S" become →"M-O-S-T"← dependent on

for the →final← "S-T-R-U-G-G-L-E"
about to "B-E-G-I-N" !!!!!!!!

March 26th, 1987.

John Inez

→"N-O ONE"← will→E-V-E-R← "KNOW" the
→"S-T-R-A-I-N"← that "TWO" "experienced" !!!!!!!
during "THEIR" →"L-O-N-G" "L-O-N-E-L-Y" "SOUL"←
finding →"T-A-S-K"← brought about
by "LIFE" →"It" "S-E-L-F who →"O-P-E-N-E-D"← !!!
the "D-O-O-R" in the "M-I-N-D" of John
"G-I-V-I-N-G" to Almighty "GOD" a →"H-U-M-A-N"←
→"form"← to "C-O-M-M-U-N-E" with thereby
making it →"P-O-S-S-I-B-L-E"← for "TWO"
to "S-H-A-R-E" a →"R-E"← kindled relationship
that →"H-A-S"← !!!!!!!!!!! "G-I-V-E-N" (→"U-N"← told)
"D-E-L-I-G-H-T" to Almighty "GOD" by
their →"U-N"← inhibited "A-P-P-R-O-A-C-H" to
an "U-N" expected →"C-A-L-L"←"I-N-G from
a →"S-U-P-E-R"← natural force known
as Life "WHO" became the "SOURCE"

responsible for "THEIR" →R-E← generation during which "TIME" Period "TWO" L-O-N-E-L-Y, "D-E-J-E-C-T-E-D", "A-P-P-R-E-H-E-N-S-I-V-E" "C-O-N-F-U-S-E-D" →&← D-I-S-T-R-E-S-S-E-D "individuals" "HAVE" stead"FASTLY" remained on →T-O-P← despite the "N-E-V-E-R" ending S-T-R-U-G-G-L-E to "B-E-A-R" up under the "S-T-R-A-I-N" "caused" by →"U-N"seen← →F-O-R-C-E-S← that "H-A-V-E" given "T-H-E-M" little →"O-R"← →"N-O"← "relief" →"making"← the over-A-L-L "T-A-S-K" one in which "TWO" "G-E-N-T-L-E, →"U-N-A-S-S-U-M-I-N-G," "C-O-N-S-I-D-E-R-A-T-E →"&"← "T-H-O-U-G-H-T-F-U-L" "individuals" →A-R-E← to shortly "B-E-G-I-N" a "journey" (that →"W-I-L-L"←) for"E-V-E-R"← "C-H-A-N-G-E" the "LIVES" of "TWO" who are being →"G-I-V-E-N"← "U-N"til Gods Putt Putts" are "S-O-U-G-H-T" out & "S-U-M-M-O-N-E-D" to

→"R-E" appear before "ONE" WHO "W-I-L-L"
become "R-E-S-P-O-N-S-I-B-L-E" for →A-L-L←
"TO" befall almighty "GOD'S" "TWO" Witnesses
following!!! "Your" upcoming →M-I-S-S-I-O-N
→&← "P-L-E-A-S-U-R-E" trip that W-I-L-L
allow "TWO" who "W-I-L-L" not only
"B-E-C-O-M-E" the "H-A-R-B-I-N-G-E-R-S"
of almighty "GOD'S" wrath but
"W-I-L-L" also "E-N-C-O-U-N-T-E-R"
"those" ("B-A-S-T-A-R-D-S")!!!!!!!!!!!!
("I-N-T-E-N-T")!!!!!!!!!!! upon ("H-O-L-D-I-N-G
THEM")!!!!!!!!!!!! "U-P" to be "M-O-C-K-E-D"
for their "S-P-O-K-E-N views" on what
almighty "GOD" "H-A-S" !!!!!!!!!!!! in
the "S-T-A-B-L-E" for →T-H-E-M← following
Father's →L-O-N-G← promised "S-A-B-B-A-T-I-C-A-L"
for "HIS" →TWO← "most L-O-V-E-D" Putt Putts
who "W-I-L-L" be →permitted← to "I-N-D-U-L-G-E"

in that which "G-I-V-E-S" "them"
(much →"J-O-Y"←) "U-N"til !!! "ONE" in whom
"will" be "L-Ō-Ō-K-E-D" on by
"T-H-O-S-E" "HYPOCRITICAL," "DOUBLE DEALING,"
"TWO FACED," →"D-A-M-N-E-D"← "B-A-S-T-A-R-D-S"
"A-S" the "S-O-U-R-C-E" "capable" of
bringing "A-B-O-U-T" →"their"← down"F-A-L-L"
by →"refusing"← to →"S-U-C-C-U-M-B"← to →"their"←
"demoralizing" →"P-L-O-Y-S"← conceived
by a "B-U-N-C-H" of ("G-O-D" →less←) !!!!!!!
"ecclesiastical" →"QUACKS"← to →"D-E-S-T-R-O-Y"←
("N-O-T only") →"T-H-E"← "ONE" "remaining"
"P-R-E-L-A-T-E" who →"O-P-E-N-E-D"← the
"D-O-O-R" in ("HIS"← mind) "TOO" !!! L-A-T-E !!!
to "KEEP" "S-A-F-E !!! Almighty "GOD'S"
"TWO" witnesses "WHO" returned to
the "S-A-N-C-T-U-A-R-Y" ???????? in
"R-E-S-P-O-N-S-E" to a "C-A-L-L"

following the T-I-M-E _period_
being →_given_← U-N _til_ "THEY" are
"M-O-V-E-D" by _Almighty_ "GOD" to
"G-E-T" "THEIR" _Final ACT_ "U-N-D-E-R" _way_
in "O-R-D-E-R" that _Almighty_ "GOD'S"
Holy Scripture be F-U-L-F-I-L-L-E-D .

May 6th, 1986.

John Inez

To →"C-O-M-P-A-R-E"← (your "C-A-L-L") with "ONE" M-A-D-E to provide Almighty "GOD" a "W-A-Y" the →"O-N-L-Y"← way He could "M-I-N-G-L-E" without disturbing (the →F-O-R-C-E responsible) for bringing →A-L-L← that "H-A-S" been →F-O-R-E← told in Holy Scripture by means of →"GOD"← / man through "A-D-O-P-T-I-N-G" (→by "C-O-N-S-E-N-T"←) TWO that →"A-L-S-O"← came into this ("LAND of E-X-I-L-E") →F-R-E-E← of →A-N-Y← guiding F-O-R-C-E to "C-O-P-E" with L-I-F-E like "K-I-N-D-R-E-D brethren →"E-N-D-E-A-V-O-R-I-N-G"← to comprehend the "M-I-N-D" →boggling← "complexities" that tend to →"R-A-T-T-L-E"← "ONES" equilibrium when "WE" have to maintain an

"O-U-T-W-A-R-D" appearance of ONE in C-O-N-T-R-O-L while "S-I-M-U-L-T-A-N-E-O-U-S-L-Y" surrendering the ("WHOLE" being) to a "I-N-V-I-S-I-B-L-E" FORCE known as "L-I-F-E"

In "OUR" (end "L-E-S-S" "Q-U-E-S-T") for "U-N-D-E-R-S-T-A-N-D-I-N-G" "WE" set about by →"O-P-E-N-I-N-G"← ("our minds") to the (→"S-O-U-R-C-E" responsible) for "A-L-L" the confusion (that →"HAS"←) influenced the "M-A-N-N-E-R" in which "WE" come to "G-R-A-S-P" with a "F-I-R-M"ness of →"P-U-R-P-O-S-E" (that →"HAS"←) "provided" "US" a "WAY" to →"C-O-M-P-A-R-E"← the →"S-T-A-T-E"← of →"L-I-F-E"← in "THREE" (that →"initially"←) "G-A-M-E" into →"B-E-I-N-G"← "E-N-D-O-W-E-D"!!! with the →"S-A-M-E"← "S-U-P-E-R" natural "P-R-O-P-E-R-T-I-E-S" belonging to "ONE"

who→"CHOSE"← ("TWO" of "HIS"→Children←)
that "S-T-R-A-Y-E-D"→"O-U-T"→side→"D-I-S"← obeying!!!
(a→House←"R-U-L-E") making "YOUR" return
(→"H-O-M-E"←) pleasing to Almighty "GOD"
who "L-O-O-K-S" on "THREE" that
"W-E-R-E" exiled in "S-I-M-I-L-A-R" fashion
to a "L-A-N-D" wherin "THEY" were
("M-A-D-E"→free←) to "CHOOSE" "THEIR"
very "O-W-N" Life "S-T-Y-L-E" making it
"P-O-S-S-I-B-L-E" for→"A-N-Y"←one to "lose"
them→"S-E-L-V-E-S"← •

March 27th, 1981.

John

Secularism holds todays GODLESS SOCIETY deeply entrenched occasioning the MORAL DECADENCE of "MAN" enslaving "ALL" whom allow THEMSELVES to become indifferent toward the worldly abandonment of much that was formerly upheld as "TRUTH".

John the TIME has COME to GIVE those who strived so diligently for SELF ACCLAIM in seeking to REMOVE every vestige relinquishing the TRADITIONAL practices universally held in "GOD'S CHURCH" in order to WEAKEN the position bestowed on those ecclesiastics delegated to SAFEGUARD the INSTITUTIONAL church from DISSENTING MILITANT individuals who received a call

from satan creating a "DIVISION" in GOD'S church that will ENDURE until the "SECOND COMING" of God's HOLY ONE The "Son of MAN" "JESUS CHRIST" regenerating in ONE who received a call from God.

John the REBELLIOUS action by a GREAT number of today's perverse "PRIESTS" defying the attempts of "THOSE PRIESTS" who are being moved by GOD to REUNITE the CHURCH have now ATTAINED that "POINT IN TIME" occasioning that which has been "PREORDAINED" rendering to "TWO who received a call from God the TASK of "FORETELLING the CALAMITIES that WILL befall ALL MANKIND".

The TASK that has been chosen for

You TWO children INEZ JOHN will CAUSE many "DISTRESS" fulfilling that which has been "FORETOLD" in Gods "Holy Scripture".

John the first ENCOUNTER involving "ONE" who has "REFUSED" to listen EXTINGUISHING THE FLAME OF CHRIST requires detachment for "TWO" of Gods children STRIVING to KEEP the FLAME OF CHRIST "BURNING WITHIN THEM bringing to a "CESSATION" the UNION intended by Jesus Christ to "SUPPORT" TWO CHOSEN by God to "FORTELL the CALAMITIES that WILL befall ALL MANKIND".

Scripture tells us that the "SECOND COMING" of Jesus Christ will be PRECEDED in "TIME" by "TWO WITNESSES" who will be "GIVEN" the KNOWLEDGE by God to PROPHECY for a

period of "FORTY TWO MONTHS" REVEALING to "ALL NATIONS" the CALAMITIES that WILL BEFALL ALL MANKIND.

The coming of the TWO WITNESSES "SIGNAL" the "forerunner" of "ALL" that "WILL" descend from a "WRATHFUL" GOD in "Retribution" for "ALL" the "HEINOUS" crimes that "HAVE" "cried" to "GOD" for "VENGEANCE" bringing through TWO "WHO WILL be DIRECTED" by Jesus Christ the "MEANS" whereby "GOD" "will" PRONOUNCE "judgement" "ON" the "WICKED" simultaneously GIVING to "those" SOULS striving to "FIND" salvation the "PROMISED WORD" of "GOD".

John the days AHEAD "are" FRAUGHT with "ANXIETIES" of a "KIND" causing "many" an "untold" HARDSHIP "creating" TROUBLES of

a "MAGNITUDE" that "WILL" ULTIMATELY "defy" "ALL" control "resulting" in the "TOTAL" collapse of a "SYSTEM" "provided" MAN by "GOD" who "LIKEWISE" "WAS" the "FORGE" "GOVERNING" to maintain "ORDER" in a "SOCIETY" "brimming" WITH "corruption", "teeming" WITH "licentiousness", "overflowing" WITH "SELF ishness" "saturated" WITH "immorality" "CONSUMED" "by" a "SELF" force "indifferent" in "THEIR" beliefs & attitudes toward ALMIGHTY "GOD" that "IS" bringing to a "CESSATION" for ("ALL TIME") the "PRESENCE" of Jesus Christ in this "LAND of EXILE" following "His" PROMISE to "give" THOSE WHO "LISTEN" the "WAY to "SALVATION as "foretold" in "HOLY SCRIPTURE" using "INEZ JOHN" as VESSELS "IN "which "GOD" "WILL" GIVE "TO" the "GENTILE" an "OPPORTUNITY" that "WILL" in "ALL" respects "EQUAL" that

which Jesus Christ "GOD" MAN gave "to" "THE" Jew "making" it "POSSIBLE" to "BELIEVE" "OR" disbelieve "that" Jesus Christ "GOD" "HAS" "returned".

JohnInez the "HOUR" "DECREED" by "GOD" is "NEAR" for "TWO" "WHO WILL" "TREAD" a "VERY" lonely "PATH" "brimming" WITH "maliciousness," "teeming" WITH "hostility," "overflowing" WITH "meanness" "saturated" WITH "evilness" CONSUMED" by a "SELF" force that "HAVE" been "TORMENTED" in "EVERY way" by "TWO" being "DIRECTED" to TELL "it" the "WAY" it "IS" by ALMIGHTY "GOD".

("JohnInez") "YOU WILL" "be PROVIDED" "FOR" in "EVERY WAY" making IT "POSSIBLE for "YOU" to "FULFILL" "ALL" that "HAS" been "DECREED" for the "TWO WITNESSES" in "God's Holy Scripture" "by"

7

God the Father God the Son God the Holy Ghost the "BLESSED TRINITY" "ALMIGHTY GOD"

PACKET #3

March 3rd, 2008

Jacob Reusner

"T-I-M-E" (→"I-S"→SHORT←) !!!!!!!!!!!! should →"WE"← "C-O-N-T-I-N-U-E" to ("H-O-L-D" →"fast"←) in the "B-E-L-I-E-F" "that" (→"Y-O-U-R" "CALLING") !!! gave "CREDENCE" to the "M-A-G-N-I-T-U-D-E" of the "T-W-O" packets →"you"← received the "N-E-E-D" to "C-O-M-P-L-Y" becomes "A-P-P-A-R-E-N-T" making (→"YOUR"← "T-A-S-K") !!! "ONE" in which →"YOU"← →Jacob Reusner← "W-I-L-L" "require" →"GOD'S"← "HELP to COMPLETE".

Jacob Reusner

"T-I-M-E" (→"I-S"→SHORT←) !!!!!!!!!!!! should →"WE"← "E-L-E-C-T" of ("OUR" "O-W-N") "free Will" to "T-A-R-R-Y" rather than "P-R-O-C-E-E-D" "WITH-O-U-T" benifit of "A-N-Y" "insider" "knowledge" "THUS" it becomes "M-O-S-T" !!!

"necessary" for "U-S" to "P-R-O-C-L-A-I-M" (to "T-H-O-S-E") that "W-I-L-L" be "G-I-V-E-N" the ("S-A-L-V-A-T-I-O-N" "message") !!!!!!!!!!!! the "M-E-A-N-S" whereby ("YOUR" "people") the "Jews" ("W-I-L-L" "know") "BEYOND" ("A-L-L" "DOUBT") the "V-A-L-I-D-I-T-Y" of ("Y-O-U-R" "C-A-L-L-I-N-G") Jacob "W-H-E-N" it "B-E-C-O-M-E-S" "C-L-E-A-R") to the "B-O-D-Y" "GOVERNING" in the ("Universal Roman Catholic Church") "THAT" !!!!!!!! ("Y-O-U-R" "MISSION") !!! !!!! "S-T-E-M-S" from "TWO" "WHO WERE" !!!!!!!! being "M-O-V-E-D" by "ONE" to "S-I-G-N-A-L" the "MANNER" in which "GOD" intends to (make "K-N-O-W-N") to "T-H-O-S-E" "P-R-E-L-A-T-E-S" having "C-L-O-U-T" within the ("I-N-N-E-R" "sanctum") of (the "D-E-S-O-L-A-T-E" "R-E-M-A-I-N-S") of the Church founded by Jesus Christ on Peter "T-H-A-T" received "letters"

from "TWO" that ("W-E-R-E" "PENNED")
by "ONE" !!!!!!!!!!!!!! "W-H-O" intends
to ("K-E-E-P" "HIS" "P-R-O-M-I-S-E") !!!!!!!!!!!!
to "Abraham" "I-N-T-A-C-T" "BY"
"G-I-V-I-N-G" !!! the "O-N-L-Y" "Jew"
"chosen" by Almighty "GOD"
the ("ONLY" "R-O-U-T-E") "that "W-I-L-L" !!!
"GIVE" Jacob & those "HE" "WILL" Choose
"P-R-O-O-F" Beyond "A-L-L" doubt the
"VALIDITY" of "your calling" through
bringing to "L-I-G-H-T" !!! copies of
"L-E-T-T-E-R-S" received pertaining to
"THOSE" Prelates within the Universal
& remnant of the Roman Catholic Church
"R-E-M-A-I-N-I-N-G" .

Jacob Neusner

"T-I-M-E" ("I-S" "SHORT") !!!!!!!!!!! should "WE"

4

"N-E-G-L-E-C-T" to "H-E-E-D" the "M-A-N-N-E-R" in which "T-H-I-S" "T-A-S-K" is to be "I-N-S-T-I-G-A-T-E-D" !!!!!!!!!!!! in order to bring "T-H-O-S-E" "WHO" "LIFE" "L-O-O-K-S" "O-N" as a "T-H-R-E-A-T" !!! to Abrahams promised message of "S-A-L-V-A-T-I-O-N" for Almighty "GOD'S" people the ("JEWS") "ON STREAM" !!! .

Jacob Neusner

In "OUR" endless "Q-U-E-S-T" to "K-E-E-P" "OUR" "B-E-L-I-E-F-S" "IN-T-A-C-T" !!!!!!!!!!!! "WE" tend to "N-E-U-T-R-A-L-I-Z-E" "OUR" "THINKING" rather than "S-T-O-P" !!!!!!! & "L-O-O-K" with an ("O-P-E-N" "DOOR") !!! in the "mind" to "A-L-L" ("THAT" "LIFE") !!! "H-A-S" !!!!!!! revealed through "letters" "THAT" "HAVE" been given "YOU" as well

as "T-H-O-S-E" which are "HEREWITH" enclosed "A-L-L" which are the "M-E-A-N-S" that, "H-A-N-D-L-E-D" !!! in the "P-R-O-P-E-R" "MANNER" "W-I-L-L" !!!!!!!!!!!! "B-E-C-O-M-E" the "K-E-Y" that "("O-P-E-N-S" the "DOOR") !!! to "S-A-L-V-A-T-I-O-N" as "PROMISED" BY Almighty "GOD" for "YOU" !!!!!!!!!!!!! & "Y-O-U-R" people THE "Jews".

Jacob Neusner

THIS "I-S" !!!!!!!!!!!! the "L-A-S-T" !!!!!!!!!!!! of ("T-H-R-E-E" "PACKETS") "YOU "W-I-L-L" be "GIVEN" leaving Jacob to "P-O-N-D-E-R" the "MANNER" in WHICH THIS ("B-U-R-D-E-N-S-O-M-E" "TASK") !!! "I-S" !!!!!!!!!!!! being "P-R-E-S-E-N-T-E-D" to Jacob Neusner the "O-N-E" & "O-N-L-Y" Jew "C-H-O-S-E-N" by

6

Almighty "GOD" to (KEEP A-L-I-V-E)!!!!!!!

(→ "HIS" ← S-A-L-V-A-T-I-O-N "message") _together_ with "HIS" ~~people~~ (THE J-E-W-S) .

JB

January 28th, 1984.

John Inez

To ("PREPARE" ONESELF) for the "UNKNOWN"!! takes ("A-L-L") of "OUR" physical & mental "RESTRAINT" directed toward the "S-O-U-R-C-E" as the ("W-A-Y" to "C-O-P-E"). with the ("U-N-E-X-P-E-C-T-E-D")!!!! "L-I-F-E" Has ("DEALT") "TWO" frail, distinctive, bewildered, distressed "personalities" (that "ARE") being "T-E-S-T-E-D" by "ONE" in "WHOM" will "H-A-V-E" to "D-E-P-E-N-D" for that ("PERIOD in TIME") in "WHICH" ("ALL" H-E-LL) "W-I-L-L" break "L-O-O-S-E" in the ("F-O-R-M-S" of "M-A-N-Y") ("BENT") on ("D-E-S-T-R-O-Y-I-N-G") the "O-N-L-Y" "VESSELS" Almighty "GOD" (HAS "C-H-O-S-E-N") for "THIS" ("Spiritual & worldly" UNDERTAKING) to be "C-O-M-F-O-R-T-A-B-L-E" in "HIS" "regenerated" V-E-H-I-C-L-E-S (that "M-U-S-T")

endure ("ANY" stressful forces "C-O-M-F-O-R-T-A-B-L-Y"
"guaranteeing" "ONE" who "HAS" ("I-N-"vested")
more "TIME" in "TWO" whose "E-L-E-V-A-T-O-R"
"is" functioning ("THROUGHOUT" ALL levels)
of ("H-U-M-A-N" mentality) bringing "US"
to that "P-O-I-N-T" in ("OUR") PREPARATION
for the "UNKNOWN"!! to ("C-R-E-A-T-E" TWO
F-O-R-M-S) in WHICH Jesus Christ ("W-I-L-L")
materialize "U-S-I-N-G" both the
"MALE" & the "FE-"MALE making it POSSIBLE
for "A-L-L" who "W-I-T-N-E-S-S" the "R-O-L-E"
being ENACTED "THROUGH" these ("TWO"
PROPHETS) of "D-E-A-T-H" ("KNOW" why)
Almighty "GOD" "chose" to "D-I-S-T-I-N-G-U-I-S-H"
between "TWO" (created) to "COMPLIMENT"
RATHER than "C-O-M-P-E-T-E" with "each" OTHER
for ("E-V-E-R-Y" position) in life "dismembering"

whatever "O-B-S-T-A-C-L-E" stands in "H-E-R"
("planned" PATH) "L-E-A-V-I-N-G" "H-I-M"
to protect "B-O-T-H"!!!!!!!

July 26th, 1984.

John Inez

Job "EPITOMIZES" human "A-T-T-I-T-U-D-E-S" when dealing with "D-I-S-T-R-E-S-S-F-U-L" situations materializing from a ("L-A-C-K") of knowledge about "GOD" creating "U-N-T-O-L-D" hardships on the "W-O-R-L-D-L-Y" (who "H-A-V-E") accepted "L-I-F-E" in (what "EV-E-R")!!! manner is "DEGREED" believing!!!!!! it is from "GOD" discovers what "T-H-E-I-R Life" purpose in ("T-H-I-S" world) is "ABOUT" enabling "THOSE" who are conscious of "RECEIVING" favors from an "UNKNOWN" God to "A-S-K" ThemSELVES "WHY"!!!! has "LIFE←LOOKED" upon "ME" rather than maintain a "P-A-T-T-E-R-N"

in keeping "T-H-A-T" which "WE" <u>have</u> been "C-O-N-D-I-T-I-O-N-E-D" by an "UNKNOWN" <u>force</u> operating ("O-U-T"side) the parameter of "U-N-D-E-R-S-T-A-N-D-I-N-G" <u>manifestations</u> arising from "O-D-D" <u>ball</u> <u>HALLUCINATIONS</u> "WE" have begun to "ACCEPT" as ("Spiritual" T-E-L-E-P-A-T-H-Y) with "GOD".

John Inez the "W-E-I-R-D" manner in which "YOUR" ~~Life~~ "STYLE" is being "HANDLED" leaves "L-O-T-S"!!!!!!! of "ROOM" to <u>doubt</u> that <u>Almighty</u> "God" would "mislead" "US" into believing WE are the "TWO WITNESSES" revealed in Holy Scripture that "WILL" become the <u>mobile</u> "PUTT PUTTS" "HOUSING" "Jesus Christ" if it were not "SO".

Strange as it "A-L-L" is "OUR" God "G-I-V-E-N" common sense "HAS" not in "A-N-Y way" indicated Spiritual "D-A-N-G-E-R" from accepting "A-L-L" "SPOKEN" thoughts "G-I-V-E-N"!!! John AS coming from Almighty "God" in spite of the "C-O-N-F-U-S-I-O-N" that "I-S" being directed "OUR" way "S-H-O-U-L-D"!!!! tell "US" that "WE" have "N-O-T"!!!!!!! been "D-E-L-U-D-E-D" by "ANY"thing .

April 7th, 1985.

John Inez

To "P-R-E-P-A-R-E" "OUR" selves for "A-L-L" that "L-I-E-S" immediately ahead WE will be required to maintain a "P-A-T-T-E-R-N" confusing!!! as "A-L-W-A-Y-S"!!! "T-R-U-S-T-I-N-G"!!! in Almighty God to "M-A-N-E-U-V-E-R" "His" TWO Putt Putts in whatever "F-A-S-H-I-O-N" is NECESSARY to bring to a "J-U-S-T" conclusion the "M-I-S-D-E-E-D-S" of "T-H-O-S-E"!!! chosen by "GOD" as "A-P-O-S-T-L-E-S" of His Son Jesus Christ "W-H-O" told "T-H-E-M" (whats "W-H-A-T")!!!! for "THEIR" salvation →"E-M-P-H-A-S-I-Z-I-N-G"← the "N-E-E-D" to "O-V-E-R-come the "F-O-R-C-E" ("predominating") in "areas" of their MAKE-UP "S-E-N-S-I-T-I-V-E"!!!

to ("T-H-E-I-R" self gratifications)!!!!!!!!!!!!
giving to "TWO" the ("J-O-I-N-T" task)!!!
of "C-A-R-R-Y-I-N-G" the "FINAL"!!! "AGT".

May 14th, 1985.

John Inez

The "M-O-M-E-N-T" is at "HAND" to "B-R-O-A-D-C-A-S-T" the ("re" B-I-R-T-H) of Jesus Christ "GOD" in the F-O-R-M-S of "HIS" "TWO" P-R-E-S-E-N-T day "witnesses" revealed in God's Holy Scripture "G-I-V-I-N-G" to "GOD" the "H-U-M-A-N" vehicles "N-E-C-E-S-S-A-R-y" to "F-R-A-T-E-R-N-I-Z-E" with "M-A-N-K-I-N-D" to "P-R-O-C-L-A-I-M" ALL that "W-I-L-L" be-"F-A-L-L" the "E-V-I-L" doer for his S-I-N-S against Almighty "GOD" WHICH has "S-E-T" the "S-T-A-G-E" for the "F-I-N-A-L" "act" for the "TWO" "Putt Putts" who "WILL" "G-O" it "A-L-O-N-E" "L-I-K-E" strangers "U-N" able to "C-O-M-P-R-E-H-E-N-D" (whats "W-H-A-T") in this "L-I-F-E" (ANY "more")

making the "J-O-B" of U-N raveling
it "A-L-L" "ONE" in which T-R-U-S-T
alone "W-I-L-L" become the "K-E-Y"
that "O-P-E-N-S" the "MIND" to
a "W-O-R-L-D" "beyond" in which
"Y-O-U" both "W-I-L-L" !!!!!!!!!!!! find
"E-T-E-R-N-A-L" BLESSEDNESS together
in "ONE" Who delights in "HIS"
Children that L-I-S-T-E-N-E-D" & "OBEYED"
the ("S-P-O-K-E-N" Mind) of Almighty "GOD".

August 28th, 1985.

John Inez

("U-N" _like_) "ALL" ("_those_" C-H-O-S-E-N) by _Almighty_ "GOD" "YOUR" calling "_requires_" an ("I-N-T-I-M-A-T-E" _knowledge_) of "God" the _Father_ ("W-H-O" _differed_) from the other ("TWO" _Members_) of the Heavenly "TRIO" "N-I-C-K" named the "H-O-L-Y" Trinity "WHERE" in ("HE") "W-A-S" the ("S-O-U-R-C-E") out of which "E-M-E-R-G-E-D" ("YOUR" _Fathers_) "TRINIT-A-R-IA-N" _make_ "U-P".

November 26th, 1985.

John Inez

"W-H-E-N" "WE" become "UP" set at CONDITIONS "over WHICH" ("WE" believe) is "OUT" side our "SCOPE" of comprehension ("S-O-M-E" relief) "C-A-N" be found through "C-H-A-N-N-E-L-L-I-N-G" what "E-V-E-R" "THOUGHTS" are given "US" in the "D-I-R-E-C-T-I-O-N" "most" likely to →"H-E-L-P"← TWO →"resign"← "THEM"selves to (→"THEIR"← L-O-T← in "LIFE"←) WHICH in the "CASE" of ("God's" →PUTT PUTTS←) "simply" "E-X-P-R-E-S-S-E-D" is Almighty "GOD" "FE-L-L-I-N-G" →"Inez John"← to (→"N-E-V-E-R"← forget) that God Your Father →"A-L-S-O"← has →"HIS"← ups & →"D-O-W-N-S"← which is a "C-O-N-S-T-A-N-T" "reminder" of →"A-L-L"← that "YOU" & "I" can "L-O-O-K" "F-O-R-W-A-R-D" to →"U-N-T-I-L"←

the →"A-C-T"← in which "TWO" "U-P" set →"L-O-N-E-L-Y"← trusting individuals "WHO" accepted a →"C-A-L-L"← to "GIVE" →"THEM" selves← to the "W-O-R-L-D" that "THIS" "final" "C-H-A-P-T-E-R" of God's Holy Scripture "B-E" fulfilled .

John Inez the "F-E-E-L-I-N-G-S" (→"W-E"← SHARE toward →"TH-O-S-E"← →"who"←"H-A-V-E" "maintained" a →"C-O-U-R-S-E"← that ("K-E-E-P-S" →"U-S"←) in a condition →"R-E-Q-U-I-R-I-N-G"← "countermeasures" of a →"N-A-T-U-R-E"← that "WILL" determine →"THEIR"← "Relationship" with →"U-S"← .

January 10th, 1986.

John

→"U-N-T-I-L"← our moment in "T-I-M-E" comes "y-o-u" together with Inez "W-I-L-L" →shortly← !!!!!!!!!!!!!! become "I-N-V-O-L-V-E-D" with "ONE" who finds "T-W-O" that ("P-O-S-S-E-S-S" knowledge) of a nature that "C-L-E-A-R-L-Y" recognizes→"A-L-L" ills (currently→"P-L-A-G-U-I-N-G"←) "T-H-O-S-E" responsible for the→"C-H-A-N-G-E-S"← that (→"are"←"T-A-K-I-N-G) !!! place "W-I-T-H-I-N" the (→"uppermost"← "O-F-F-I-C-E") "entrusted" to ("P-R-E-S-E-R-V-E"→"TRADITION"←) !!!!!!!!!!!!!! that→"G-A-V-E"← the →"MYSTICAL B-O-D-Y"← of ("GOD'S"→temple←) S-U-B-S-T-A-N-C-E giving the "T-R-A-D-I-O-N-A-L-I-S-T-S" →"M-A-N-Y"← ways to "C-O-M-M-U-N-E"

with "GOD" for →A-L-L← their "N-E-E-D-S".

JohnInez

"Y-O-U-R" period of "S-E-C-L-U-S-I-O-N"
"W-I-L-L" "E-N-D" the →"DAY"← you both
"R-E-T-U-R-N" to the →"S-A-N-C-T-U-A-R-Y"←
that →"H-A-S"← kept "S-A-F-E" "ONE" in
"WHOM" will →view← "TWO" with
→"G-R-E-A-T"← puzzlement following "y-o-u-r"
"S-A-D-D-L-E-I-N-G" the "REBEL" responsible
for holding "F-A-S-T" to the only →"T-R-U-E"←
remnant of God's Church remaining
with a →"R-E-A-L"← heavy in the
form of "C-O-R-R-E-S-P-O-N-D-E-N-C-E"
directed to →THOSE← "WHO" Almighty "GOD"
→"H-A-S"← ("Given "UP") on for →"T-H-E-I-R"←
failure to ("O-V-E-R" come) the →"S-E-L-F"← force
controlling "THEM".

April 22nd, 1984.

Easter Tiding

John & Inez

To-day is the "R-E-S-U-R-R-E-C-T-I-O-N" of a "L-I-F-E" sustaining "F-O-R-C-E" being "G-I-V-E-N" by Almighty "GOD" to "M-A-N-K-I-N-D" for the "L-A-S-T" brief period in the (allotted "T-I-M-E" Span) given T-W-O chosen for their "M-A-K-E up" to become the ("H-U-M-A-N" forms) in which "Jesus Christ" ("I-S" using) to Signal the "M-A-N-N-E-R" by which GOD "W-I-L-L" "make known" to the ("J-E-W-I-S-H" people) the "M-Y-S-T-E-R-Y" surrounding the GOD/man

Jesus Christ

November 19th, 1986.

John & Inez

"H-E-L-P" is on the way for "TWO"
"lonely" "C-O-N-F-U-S-E-D" "discouraged"
"disconsolate" "W-E-A-R-Y" "downtrodden"
→"MORTALS"← who "V-I-E-W" "Life" with
"S-O-M-E" "U-N" certainty regarding "U-N" fulfilled
→"P-R-O-M-I-S-E-S"← that "H-A-V-E" tormented
"TWO" who "W-E-R-E" being →"P-R-E-S-S-U-R-E-D"←
to →"R-E-J-E-C-T"← the "B-E-L-I-E-F" that
Almighty "GOD" would "ACT" in a
manner "C-O-N-T-R-A-R-Y" to "A-L-L" "we"
"H-A-V-E" been "C-O-N-D-I-T-I-O-N-E-D" to
"accept" as the "O-N-L-Y" way in which
"GOD" speaks to "M-A-N-K-I-N-D" when in
→"R-E-A-L-I-T-Y"← "YOUR" Father "D-I-S-C-I-P-L-I-N-E-S"
"HIS" →Very Own "V-E-S-S-E-L-S"← in

"W-H-A-T" →ever← !!!!!!!!!!!! fashion to
be "C-E-R-T-A-I-N" "THEY" W-I-L-L →"HOLD" fast←
to "T-H-A-T" which "you" both BELIEVE
→"R-E-G-A-R-D-L-E-S-S"← !!!!!!!!!!!!!

February 8th, 1988.

John Inez

In the "B-E-G-I-N-N-I-N-G" (→"you"← chose) to follow the "S-P-O-K-E-N WORD" of an "I-N-V-I-S-I-B-L-E" force at work in the "M-I-N-D" of John who initially →"A-C-C-E-P-T-E-D"← the →"S-U-P-E-R"← natural →"C-A-L-L"← with"O-U-T" B-E-N-I-F-I-T of some →"P-R-O-O-F"← that "ONE" could "L-O-O-K" on as coming from "ABOVE" that would ("G-I-V-E" them) a "W-A-Y" to →"P-E-R-C-E-I-V-E"← the →"R-E-A-L"← existence of a "S-U-B-L-I-M-I-N-A-L" force "C-A-L-L-E-D" "God" who "I-S"!!! the "ONE" responsible for "S-T-I-R-R-I-N-G" "YOU" both to a "C-O-N-D-I-T-I-O-N" of ("TOTAL" →"un"← R-E-S-I) both in mind

& Spirit in O-R-D-E-R to "P-R-E-P-A-R-E" "His" (=TWO Putt Putts=) for the "O-P-E-N" confrontation with "P-O-S-I-T-I-V-E" (=thinking= ???) members of the "E-X-C-O-M-M-U-N-I-C-A-T-E-D" remnant of "God's" Church who W-I-L-L use "THEIR" →"S-E-L-F"← taught religious "A-C-U-M-E-N" concerning Almighty "GOD" & "HIS" "Modus Operandi" to →"D-I-S-P-R-O-V-E"= !!! "ANY" thought →you← receive concerning almighty "GOD" in →"O-R-D-E-R"← to→"P-R-O-V-E"=!!! unequivocally to ("TWO" Prelates) "G-I-V-E-N" a Spiritual →"J-O-L-T"= !!!!!!! the "I-M-P-I-O-U-S" Life "S-T-Y-L-E" of "TWO" distraught, imaginative, earthy, unfulfilled ("middle aged") individuals ("WHO" have) "L-O-S-T" touch with R-E-A-L-I-T-Y is →"P-O-S-S-E-S-S-E-D"= by their →"U-N"= earthly

3

"B-E-L-I-E-F" that almighty "GOD" "H-A-S" revealed to "THEM" their →"S-C-R-I-P-T-U-R-A-L"← role as ("HIS" mouth P-I-E-C-E)→"H-E-R-E"← on "EARTH" delineating "THEM" as "God L-I-K-E" in "T-H-E-I-R" new "F-O-U-N-D" transcendental "A-P-P-R-O-A-C-H" to "T-H-O-S-E" holding "P-O-S-I-T-I-O-N-S" of "AUTHORITY" within the Church through "THEIR" "UN-C-A-N-N-Y"← ability to "R-E-A-D" situations without "B-E-N-I-F-I-T" of →"A-N-Y"← insider "K-N-O-W-L-E-D-G-E".

May 23rd, 1989.

John Inez

"F-U-T-I-L-I-T-Y" best describes the "E-X-E-R-C-I-S-E" undertaken by Almighty "GOD" to keep afloat the "V-E-S-S-E-L" "established" in a "L-A-N-D" (that "H-A-S" become) !!!!!!! the "C-E-S-S-P-O-O-L" of "iniquity" "M-A-D-E" to "H-O-L-D" & provide "A-L-L" those "E-X-P-E-L-L-E-D" from God's "R-E-A-L-M" with "E-V-E-R-Y" opportunity to "F-I-N-D" a "Spiritual" "H-A-V-E-N" that "W-O-U-L-D" "guarantee" ("ANY" soul) "L-O-O-K-I-N-G" to find "S-A-L-V-A-T-I-O-N" a "C-O-V-E-N-A-N-T" given "MAN" by "GOD".

John Inez

"H-O-P-E-L-E-S-S" is "A-N" other "WORD" that "S-U-M-S" up Almighty "GOD'S" thought toward "A-N-Y" one "L-I-S-T-E-N-I-N-G" much less "B-E-L-I-E-V-I-N-G" in "TWO" Spiritual "L-O-W" Lifes "W-H-O" view them S-E-L-V-E-S as Almighty "GOD'S" chosen harbingers of the "S-P-O-K-E-N" word when in "R-E-A-L-I-T-Y" "THEY" the "elect" !!! as "A-L-W-A-Y-S" !!!!!!! have "THEIR" ??? "God" "A-L-T-O-G-E-T-H-E-R" .

May 11th, 1994.

John Inez

Immortality "O-V-E-R-C-O-M-E-S" the manner in which we "A-D-D-R-E-S-S" our role in Life's→"C-A-L-L-I-N-G"← in order to D-E-F-I-N-E the necessity to change in those areas of →"S-E-L-F"← conflict that tend to neutralize our rationale negating those →"S-P-E-C-I-A-L"← qualities that "SEPERATE" U-S from →"A-L-L"← !!! others.

John →"Y-O-U-R"← !!! calling is that of "O-N-E" who becomes the "M-O-D-E" through which →"A-L-L"← that →"W-I-L-L"← descend from O-N high.

Inez →"Y-O-U-R"← !!! calling requires

you to become the foundation upon
which _ALLMIGHTY_ "God" _must_ →rely←.

John Inez "_YOUR_" Father ="W-I-L-L"= !!!!!!!
maintain "HIS" Life support in "ONE" who
"_H-A-S_" !!! supported you during a most
distressing period in "_YOUR_" Spiritual "W-A-L-K"
in return by WAY of making _HER_
physical recovery ="C-O-M-P-L-E-T-E"= !!!

July 5th, 1983.

"POPE" JOHN PAUL II

"V-E-R-S-U-S"

JESUS "CHRIST"

(The ("F-I-N-A-L" CHAPTER) in the "W-O-R-L-D".)

Since the BEGINNING "M-A-N" HAS C-H-O-S-E-N
to travel a "P-A-T-H" proportional to the
("F-O-R-C-E of S-E-L-F") "GROWING" causing
"S-O-C-I-E-T-Y" to "S-I-N-K" beyond ("A-L-L")
"RESTORATION" DISMEMBERING the "R-O-U-T-E"
CHRIST ("P-L-A-N-N-E-D") to PREPARE ("T-H-O-S-E"
SENTENCED) to this ("LAND" of E-X-I-L-E)
preventing "T-R-A-D-I-T-I-O-N" which ("HISTORIANS"
tell US) ("M-A-R-K-S" the "O-U-T-S-E-T") of

("MANS" S-O-J-O-U-R-N) in ("TIME") instituting a (M-Y-S-T-I-C-A-L "BODY") in the "FORM" of "ONE" invested with ("A-L-L") HUMAN T-R-A-I-T-S creating the ("M-E-D-I-U-M") through which Jesus "CHRIST" ("W-I-L-L" MATERIALIZE) to ("C-O-M-B-A-T") "MAN" for ("A-L-L") his injustices to almighty "GOD" whose ("ONLY" C-R-I-M-E) was to (come "D-O-W-N") to this ("L-O-U-S-Y") →planet← to be ("rejected") & (pinned to a "G-I-B-B-E-T") by a ("S-E-L-F" possessed) ("S-E-L-F" CONDEMNED←) ("MULTITUDE") of ("W-I-C-K-E-D" CREATURES) WHO (T-R-A-V-E-R-S-E "TIME") ("D-I-S-G-U-I-S-E-D") in ("S-E-L-F" righteousness) that ("S-P-E-A-K") with a ("F-O-R-C-E-F-U-L" tongue) ("U-S-I-N-G the P-O-W-E-R") of ("P-O-S-I-T-I-O-N") to bring to pass ("A-L-L") that ("O-N-E") elects .

Since the BEGINNING "M-A-N" (HAS chosen) to ("R-E-L-Y" on the "S-E-L-F" force) to (OVERCOME "A-L-L") that (C-O-M-E-S "our" W-A-Y) effecting the "OUTCOME" of ("MANS" S-O-J-OU-R-N) in ("TIME") ("ENDING") the ("T-O-R-R-E-N-T") of ("A-B-O-M-I-N-A-B-L-E" CRIMES) perpetrated against Almighty "GOD" by A-L-L (WHOM "H-A-V-E") allowed the ("S-E-L-F" FOUNDATION) to ("R-O-T") beyond "S-A-L-V-A-T-I-O-N".

The "W-O-R-L-D" has "E-N-T-E-R-E-D" into judgment following the ("T-I-M-E") GRACIOUSLY given A-L-L "WHO" (D-E-S-C-E-N-D-E-D) to this (L-A-N-D of E-X-I-L-E) for "THEIR" "SINFUL ACT" against Almighty "GOD" bringing to a "CONCLUSION" the ("FINAL" C-H-A-P-T-E-R) in ("MANS" S-T-R-U-G-G-L-E) to ("C-O-N-T-R-O-L") the ("F-O-R-C-E" responsible) for GIVING "H-I-M" A-L-L "H-E" BELIEVES "S-E-L-F"

is (ENTITLED TO "R-E-GA-R-D-L-E-S-S") of
WHAT WA-S told him ("W-O-U-L-D" COME) his way
"S-H-O-U-L-D" "H-E" FAIL to "H-E-E-D" that WHICH
"S-C-R-I-P-T-U-R-E" revealed through ("T-H-O-S-E")
"WHO" WERE being "D-I-R-E-C-T-E-D" by Almighty GOD
AS WELL AS receiving the "S-P-O-K-E-N" W-O-R-D
of "ONE" who "WAS" REJECTED & "P-I-N-N-E-D"
to a "G-I-B-B-E-T" by THE "S-E-L-F" righteous
"S-E-L-F" condemned "WHO" T-R-A-V-E-R-S-E TIME
C-L-O-T-H-E-D in (fanciful "A-T-T-I-R-E") THAT
"H-A-V-E" "G-I-V-E-N" (them "S-E-L-V-E-S") to
"P-E-R-D-I-T-I-O-N" through "T-H-E-I-R" inability
to "C-O-N-T-R-O-L" the S-E-L-F FORCE that
(D-E-C-I-D-E-S "OUR" D-E-S-T-I-N-Y).

"MAN" has "R-E-A-C-H-E-D" the "E-N-D" of
T-I-M-E extended the ("IN-H-U-M-A-N-E")
(WHO "S-A-T-U-R-A-T-E") this "LAND" of "D-O-O-M"

5

"P-R-E-P-A-R-E-D" by ONE to "C-A-P-T-U-R-E"
("ANY") (that "E-V-E-R") allowed the
("force" of "S-E-L-F") to (remain in "C-O-N-T-R-O-L")
("W-I-L-L" SHORTLY !!!) "E-X-P-E-R-I-E-N-C-E" the
("full" MEASURE) of Almighty "GOD'S" WRATH
through the "T-R-A-N-S-F-I-G-U-R-A-T-I-O-N".

There is "ONE" ("S-E-L-F" righteous "P-R-E-L-A-T-E")
adorned in "R-A-I-N-M-E-N-T" (un "WORTHY" !!!)
"WHO" S-T-A-N-D-S ("S-E-L-F" convinced) HE
is "T-H-E O-N-E" to O-V-E-R-C-O-M-E the ("ILLS")
"O-P-P-R-E-S-S-I-N-G" (HIS) fellow "C-O-U-N-T-R-Y" men
"C-L-O-A-K-E-D" as the ("FISHER of MEN") "using" !!!
Almighty "GOD" & the D-E-S-O-L-A-T-E D-E-B-R-I-S
(that "W-A-S") "HIS" (D-O-M-A-I-N) "established"
at the ("S-A-C-R-I-F-I-C-I-A-L" cost) of "ONE"
"WHO" promised to return to "F-O-R-E-T-E-L-L"
"MAN" of his ("J-U-S-T" REVENGE) in

retribution (together "WITH") "HIS" promised
("SALVATION" E-X-H-O-R-T-A-T-I-O-N) wrapping "UP"
The ("F-I-N-A-L" CHAPTER) in the "W-O-R-L-D" following
the ("O-P-E-N" conflict) ("BETWEEN") O-N-E called

"POPE" JOHN PAUL II

"D-E-F-E-N-D-A-N-T" (in "W-O-R-K-S") "A-N-T-I"

JESUS "CHRIST"

(WHICH "W-I-L-L") involve ("A-L-L") ("L-I-V-I-N-G"
BEINGS) (effecting) the ("C-O-U-R-S-E"
initiated) by (all) W-H-O-M "REGARDED"
the "ADVENT" of the "INCARNATION" as a
("S-T-O-R-Y") concocted to "S-P-U-R" the
("S-E-L-F" force) controlling MAN to (TREAD a
"P-A-T-H") that ("W-O-U-L-D") exert "RE-L-I-G-I-O-U-S

7

BELIEF" (keeping "T-H-O-S-E") WHO ("T-R-A-V-E-R-S-E"
TIME) believing in the "E-X-T-R-A-T-E-R-E-S-T-R-I-A-L"
existence of a "S-U-P-R-E-M-E BEING" (WHO
"W-I-L-L") come to GIVE ("S-I-N-N-E-R-S")
("E-T-E-R-N-A-L" punishment) at the "S-A-M-E" TIME
"R-E-W-A-R-D-I-N-G" (ALL) "T-H-O-S-E" faithful
("&") ("S-E-L-F" righteous) "Z-E-A-L-O-T-S" (WHO)
disM-E-M-B-E-R the ("C-H-U-R-C-H") established
in a L-A-N-D where the ("M-I-N-O-R-I-T-Y" RULE)
"C-L-O-A-K-E-D" in (what"EVER") ("MASK") is
"D-E-E-M-E-D" to be successful in the
"P-U-R-S-U-I-T" of (any"THING") (ONE"self" "DESIRES")
("I-R-R-E-S-P-E-C-T-I-V-E") of (WHAT"ONES') "C-O-N-S-C-I-E-N-C-E"
is dictating ("S-H-A-C-K-L-I-N-G" many)
"POWERLESS" to find the "S-O-L-U-T-I-O-N"
WHILE punishing ALL "LOOKING" to the
"SELF" force to "J-U-S-T-I-F-Y" (THEIR "W-O-R-K-S") .

JC

October 25th, 2007.

Inez John

"Y-O-U-R" "Calling" is "L-O-O-K-E-D" on by Almighty "GOD" as "ONE" in which "TWO" "U-N" usual "U-N" expected & "U-N" forgetable "individuals" "C-H-O-S-E-N" for "their" "M-A-K-E-U-P" to "B-E-C-O-M-E" (as "ONE" in "THEIR" "R-O-L-E") enabling "THEM" to "complete" the "T-A-S-K" that "W-I-L-L" "require" a ("FIRMNESS" of "PURPOSE") to ("O-V-E-R-C-O-M-E" "A-L-L" "O-B-S-T-A-C-L-E-S") that "W-I-L-L" "C-O-N-F-R-O-N-T" "T-H-E-M" "T-H-R-O-U-G-H-O-U-T" ("THEIR" "T-I-M-E" "H-E-R-E") "P-E-N-D-I-N-G" the "O-U-T come" of a ["C-O-L-O-S-S-A-L" "POWER" struggle] "BETWEEN" "T-W-O" "OPPOSING" "F-A-C-T-I-O-N-S" "HEADED" by "O-N-E" "I-N-T-E-N-T" ON

2

"DESTROYING" "TWO" for "THEIR" REFUSAL TO "S-U-C-C-U-M-B" to the "D-E-M-O-R-A-L-I-Z-I-N-G" PLOYS) of THOSE "S-E-L-F" righteous "intellectually" "E-N-D-O-W-E-D" "HYPOCRITICAL" ("F-L-O-C-K" of "A-S-S-H-O-L-E-S") "WHO" believe "THEY" have Almighty "GOD" Altogether "W-I-L-L" "SHORTLY" "BECOME" the "T-A-R-G-E-T" of (Almighty "GODS" "W-R-A-T-H"-ful "vengeance") in "R-E-T-U-R-N" for "A-L-L" the "A-B-O-M-I-N-A-B-L-E" "C-R-I-M-E-S" "WHICH" "H-A-V-E" "caused" the "L-O-S-S" of an "UNTOLD" number of "S-O-U-L-S" "WHICH" "W-E-R-E" (the "P-R-O-P-E-R-T-Y" "B-E-L-O-N-G-I-N-G") "T-O" the "O-N-E" "WHO" "I-N-T-E-N-D-S" to "MAKE" "A-L-L" "regardless" of their "P-O-S-I-T-I-O-N" on the "ecclesiastical" "L-A-D-D-E-R" in the "U-N-I-V-E-R-S-A-L" "Roman Catholic Church" that "O-P-T-E-D"

for the "E-C-U-M-E-N-I-C-A-L" "PUSH"
GIVING "Jesus Christ" ("MANKIND'S"
"O-N-L-Y" "R-E-D-E-E-M-E-R") the
"B-O-O-T" from "H-I-S" "TEMPLE"
"S-O-L-E-L-Y" to "A-P-P-E-A-S-E" a "L-A-R-G-E"
"BODY" of "S-E-L-F" called "Christian sects"?
know "THAT" after "2000 Y-E-A-R-S" !!!
of "W-A-T-C-H-I-N-G" the "D-E-S-T-R-U-C-T-I-O-N"
of the "O-N-L-Y" "TEMPLE" founded by
Jesus Christ on Peter by a "B-L-I-N-D"
"S-T-U-P-I-D" "UN-G-O-D-L-Y" "U-S-E-L-E-S-S"
"F-L-O-C-K" of "A-S-S-H-O-L-E-S" reached
their "C-L-I-M-A-X" at the "A-D-V-E-N-T"
of "V-A-T-I-C-A-N" II "W-H-E-N" !!!!!!!
"THEY" "removed" Almighty "GOD'S"
promised message of "S-A-L-V-A-T-I-O-N"
to "ABRAHAM" for "HIS" people the "JEWS"
"A-L-L" because the "S-E-L-F" force

"controlling" "Y-O-U" "DUMB" "S-H-I-T-S"
"elected" to "S-U-C-C-U-M-B" to "THOSE"
Religious "S-E-C-T-S" that "WILL NEVER"
change "B-E-C-A-U-S-E" they "L-O-O-K-E-D"
on the "TRANSUBSTANTIATION" as
"H-E-L-D" in the Roman Catholic Church
"N-O-T-H-I-N-G" !!!!!!! more than an "extreme"
"R-I-T-E" unacceptable to "THEM" in
its "original" "C-O-N-C-E-P-T" which
ultimately became the "R-O-O-T" responsible
for the Presiding "H-E-A-D" of "GOD'S" "TEMPLE"
"L-O-O-K-I-N-G" for "UNAMINITY" together
with "A-L-L" Sects "USING" "S-H-I-T" in lieu
of "GOD" Given "COMMON SENSE" for
"BRAINS" By casting "HIS" lot with
them using "VATICAN II" as the
means whereby "Jesus Christ" was
given the unceremonious "B-O-O-T"

from "H-I-S" "OWN TEMPLE" bringing to "A-L-L" !!!!!!! THOSE "useless" "A-S-S-H-O-L-E-S" "H-O-L-D-I-N-G" positions of authority in the "D-E-S-O-L-A-T-E" "remains" of the Church founded by "Jesus Christ" on "Peter" "W-I-L-L" !!! "S-H-O-R-T-L-Y" "B-E-C-O-M-E" the "TARGET" of Almighty G-O-D'S "F-U-L-L" Wrath W-H-E-N "Jesus Christ" "RETURNS" TO "H-I-S" "Church" for the "L-A-S-T" "TIME" in the "F-O-R-M-S" of Almighty "G-O-D'S" "TWO" "WITNESSES" TO "B-O-O-T" "YOU" "A-L-L" !!!!!! "INTO" "H-E-L-L" IN "R-E-T-U-R-N" ● !!!!!!!

The "Genesis" of God / MAN

Jesus "Christ" (WAS) a

"H-U-M-A-N" manifestation of Almighty "GOD" invested with ("ALL") human "TRAITS" "T-H-U-S" placing "GOD" made / man in a "L-A-N-D" where "HIS" ORIGIN had been "concealed" from "HIM" by GOD / The Father "WHOSE" purpose was to ("O-V-E-R-C-O-M-E") as "man" ("A-L-L") temptations "E-X-P-E-R-I-E-N-C-E-D" by "humankind" for ("T-H-E-I-R" !!! S-I-N) against Almighty "GOD" as well as being "GIVEN" the (burdensome "T-A-S-K") of comprehending "both" "HIS" (DIVINITY & purpose)